Competitive games for your everyday handball training
60 exercises for every age group

Introduction

Handball needs quick and correct decisions in each game situation. This can be trained playfully and diversely through handball-specific games. These 60 exercises are divided into seven categories and train the playing skills.

The book deals with the following subjects:
- Team ball variants
- Team play with different targets
- Tag games
- Sprint and relay race games
- Ball throwing and transportation games
- Games from other types of sports
- Complex closing game variants

The exercises are illustrated and described in an easy, comprehensible manner. They can be immediately integrated in every training unit. Various difficulty levels, additional notes, and possible variations allow for adjustment to each age group and group size.

Sample figure:

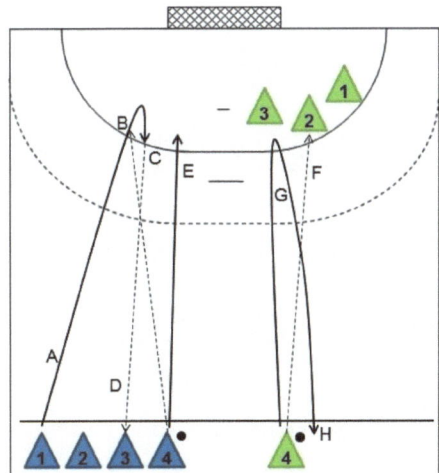

1st English edition released on 31 Mar 2017
German original edition released on 18 Sep 2015

Published by DV Concept
Editors, Design and Layout: Jörg Madinger, Elke Lackner
Proofreading and English translation: Nina-Maria Nahlenz

ISBN: 978-3-95641-184-7

The book and its contents are protected by copyright. No reprinting, photomechanical reproduction, storing or processing in electronic systems without the publisher's written permission.

Competitive games for your everyday handball training
60 exercises for every age group

Contents:

No.	Name	Players	Difficulty level	Page
Category: Team ball variants				
1	Team ball: Basic version and variant	6	★	5
2	Team ball with additional running exercises	6	★	6
3	Team ball with moving 1	8	★	7
4	Team ball with mats	8	★	8
5	Team ball with hoops	8	★	9
6	Team ball with boxes	8	★	10
7	Team ball with 4 targets	8	★	11
8	Power team ball	8	★	12
9	Team ball on four side lines	12	★★	13
10	Team ball with subsequent action	10	★★	14
11	Team ball with two different exercises	12	★★	15
12	Team ball with subsequent exercise	16	★★	16
13	Team ball with change of playing field	8	★★	17
14	Team ball with fast break	9	★★	19
15	Team ball with cone goals and team exercise	8	★★	20
16	Team ball with moving 2	8	★★	21
Category: Team play with different targets				
17	Bucket ball	8	★	22
18	Pyramid ball	6	★	23
19	Pass to player behind the line	10	★	24
20	Kempa with safety mat	8	★	25
21	Playing with 3 vaulting boxes	8	★	26
22	Touch ball with safety mat	8	★★	27
23	Diagonal team ball in 4 teams	10	★★	28
24	Laying down the ball and bridging playing fields	10	★★	29
25	3:2-outnumbered competition	12	★★	30
26	Dice ball with additional exercise	10	★★	31
Category: Tag games				
27	Tag rally	6 (12)	★	33
28	Team tag on two fields	10	★	34
29	Sprint competition with playing cards	6	★	35
30	Chasing competition	6	★	36
31	Rope tag	8	★	37
32	"Ball holding means safe" play tag	9	★★	37
33	Play tag with ball	8	★★	38
34	1-on-1 play tag	6	★★	39

No.	Name	Players	Difficulty level	Page
Category: Sprint and relay race games				
35	Game of pairs with sprint	6	★	40
36	Sprint course with playing cards	6	★	41
37	Medicine ball relay race	3	★	42
38	"Going to Jerusalem" rope skipping	6	★	43
39	Collecting playing cards and throwing at the basket	6	★	44
40	Corner sprint on command	6	★	45
41	Sprint competition with two groups and different exercises	10	★★	46
42	Team pendulum relay race	8	★★	47
43	Sprint relay race with passing	8	★★	48
44	Coordination sprint competition	8	★★	49
45	Medicine ball transportation with sprint relay race	8	★★★	50
Category: Ball throwing and transportation games				
46	Ball throwing competition	8	★	51
47	Pushing the ball	6	★	52
48	Transportation relay race	6	★	53
49	Ball transportation and shooting	8	★	54
50	Ball transportation by passing	12	★	55
Category: Games from other types of sports				
51	Soccer in pairs	8	★★	56
52	No-look ball	6	★★	57
53	2-on-2 intensive soccer variant	12	★★	58
54	Endurance run with basketball	8	★★	59
55	Dribbling-and-passing soccer	8	★★	60
Category: Complex closing game variants				
56	Competition with defensive/offensive action	9	★★	61
57	3-on-3 with running player	14	★★	62
58	Competition with defensive/offensive action 2	12	★★	63
59	Handball with team completion	11	★★	64
60	Beach handball variant	12	★★	65

Editor's note

Further reference books published by DV Concept

Competitive games for your everyday handball training
60 exercises for every age group

 handball-uebungen.de

Key:

No. of exercise   Name of exercise   Minimum number of players

No. 1	Team ball: Basic version and variant	6	★
Equipment required:	1 handball, 4 cones, playing field suitable for number of players		

✗	Cone	
 ▮▮	Small gym mat	Difficulty level
▮	Safety mat	Easy: ★
		Medium: ★★
		Difficult: ★★★
 ⦿	Ball box	
 ▬	Small vaulting box	
 ▬	Large vaulting box	
 ▢	Small vaulting box, upside down	
 ○	Hoop, bucket	
 ●●●	Medicine ball, soft ball, tennis ball, soccer ball	
▬	Balance bench	
 △	Handball pyramid	
 ◼	Dice	
 ▭▭▭▭	Coordination ladder	
 ═	Bars	
ᑲ	Basketball basket	

Competitive games for your everyday handball training
60 exercises for every age group

Category: Team ball variants

No. 1	Team ball: Basic version and variant	6	★
Equipment required:	1 handball, 4 cones, playing field suitable for number of players		

Setting:
- Define a suitable field with cones (suitable for the number of players and their level of performance).
- Make two teams.

Course (figure 1):
- The team who has the ball tries to play a certain number of passes (5/10) while trying to keep the players of the defending team from touching the ball (A).
- If they manage to play the defined number of passes, they get a point and the other team gets the ball.
- The team who has the fewest points at the end must do a predefined exercise (2 accelerating runs, for example).

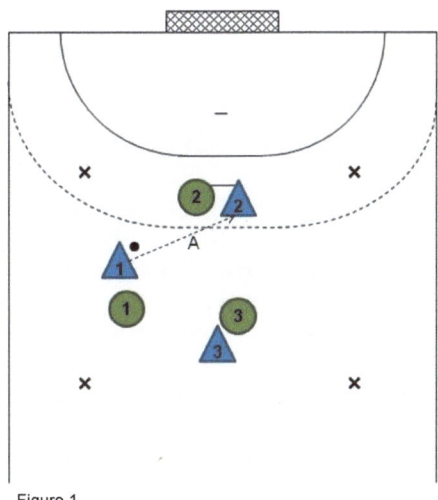

Figure 1

Variant (figure 2):
- The team only gets a point if the player (1 here) who played a pass (A) to his teammate (2) receives the ball again immediately (C) – return pass.
- For this purpose, 1 must get into space immediately after he played the pass (B).
- Passing to another teammate (3) (D) is also allowed; the players do not get a point for this however.

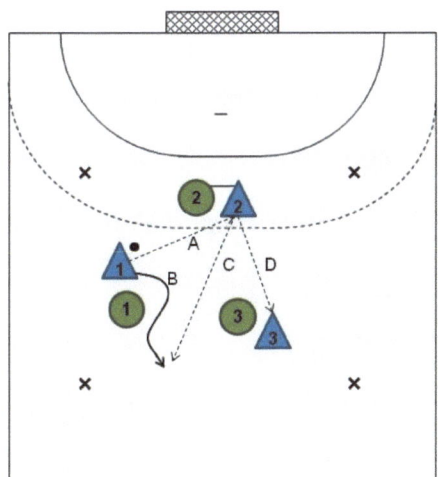

Figure 2

No. 2	Team ball with additional running exercises	6	★
Equipment required:	1 handball, 4 cones, playing field suitable for number of players		

Setting:
- Define a suitable field with cones (suitable for the number of players and their level of performance).
- Make two teams.

Course 1 (figure 1) (6-8 players):
- The teams play team ball in the playing field (see exercise no. 1).
- After each pass (A), the players must run around a cone first (B) before they may receive a pass again. If the team who has the ball manages to play 10 passes without the other team touching the ball, the defending players must do 10 quick jumping jacks, for example.
- Without dribbling.

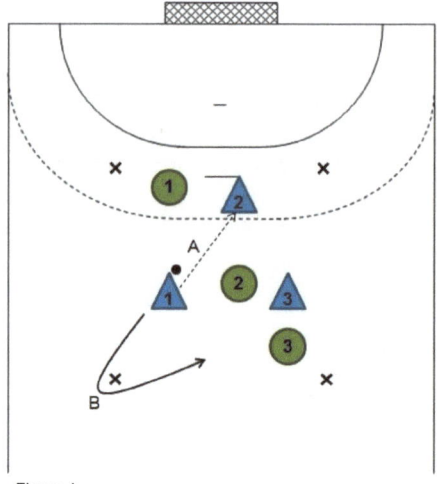
Figure 1

Course 2 (figure 2) (8 or more players):
- The players play on the entire half of the court.
- Following each pass, ▲1 must leave the playing field first (A) before he may receive a pass again.
- If the team who has the ball manages to play 10 passes without the other team touching the ball, the defending team must do 10 quick jumping jacks, for example.
- Without dribbling.

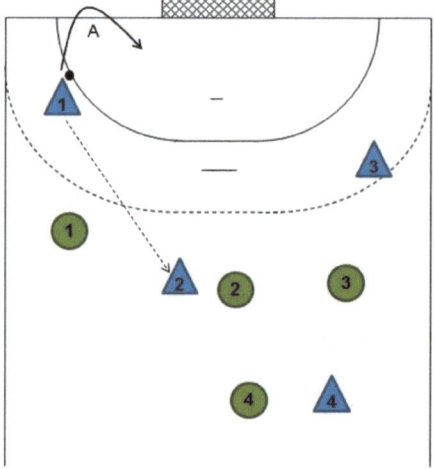
Figure 2

Additional exercises for the players who left the field after playing the pass before they are allowed to step back into the field and receive a pass again (exercises must be done outside of the field):
- 5 push-ups, 1 somersault on a mat, 5 straight jumps, for example.

No. 3	Team ball with moving 1	8	★
Equipment required:	1 handball, 4 cones, playing field suitable for number of players		

Setting:
- Divide the playing field into four smaller fields using cones (I to IV).
- Make two teams.

Course:
- The two teams play team ball against each other.
- The player holding the ball must dribble out of his field first (A and B) before he is allowed to play a pass.

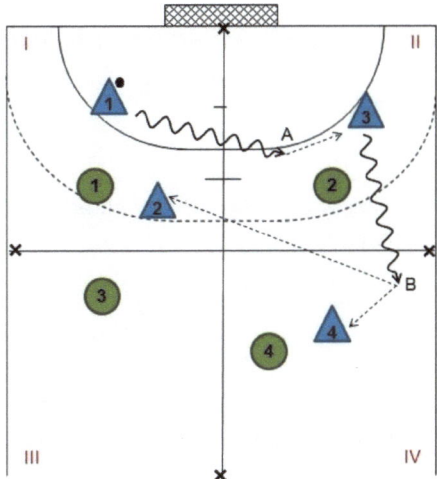

Exercise/objective:
- The attacking players try to play 10 passes. If they succeed, the defending players must do a predefined exercise.

Variants:
- No return passes allowed (for larger groups).
- Jump shot passes.
- Passing with the non-throwing hand.

No. 4	Team ball with mats	8	★
Equipment required:	When playing 4-on-4, 6 mats required (2 more mats than players per team), 1 handball, ½ handball court or equivalent playing field		

Setting:
- Put several gym mats on the floor of the playing field.
- Make two teams.

Course:
- The teams play team ball against each other.
- The players get a point, if they manage to play a pass to their teammate standing on the mat (A).
- They do not get the point, if a player of the other team touches the mat (B), but are allowed to continue.
- Dribbling is allowed.

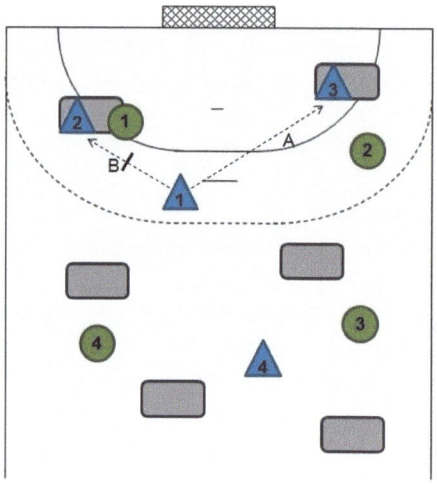

Exercise/objective:
- The attacking players try to score 10 points. If they succeed, the defending players must do a predefined exercise.
- The players are not allowed to play passes from one mat to another mat; they must leave the mat first or play a pass to one of the players not standing on a mat.

Variants:
- Without dribbling.
- No return passes.
- Jump shot passes.
- Passing with the non-throwing hand.

No. 5	Team ball with hoops	8	⭐
Equipment required:	1 handball, 2 more hoops than players per team, playing field suitable for number of players		

Setting:
- Make two teams.
- Put the hoops on the floor of the playing field (two more hoops than players per team).

Course:
- Two teams play team ball in the playing field.
- The players score a point, if the player receiving the pass stands in a hoop with one foot (A).
- They do not get a point, if a player of the other team stands in the hoop as well (B).

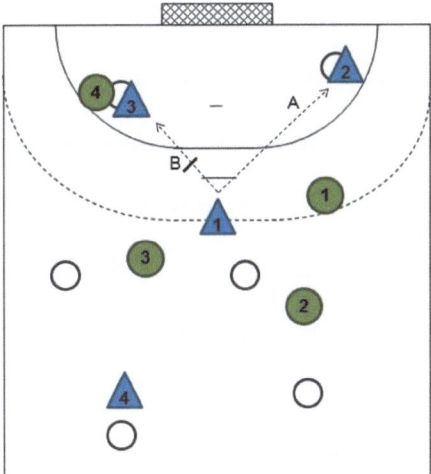

Variants:
- The player must not only stand in the hoop, but also bounce the ball on the floor inside the hoop one time.

⚠ Make sure the distance between the hoops is not too long, so that the game becomes faster.

⚠ You need at least one or two more hoops than players per team, since otherwise, the defending players are able to block them all.

Competitive games for your everyday handball training
60 exercises for every age group

No. 6	Team ball with boxes	8	★
Equipment required:	1-2 more boxes than players per team (in the example: 4 players and 5 boxes), 1 handball, playing field suitable for number of players		

Setting:
- Make two teams.
- Put small vaulting boxes (at least one more than players per team) on the floor of the playing field.

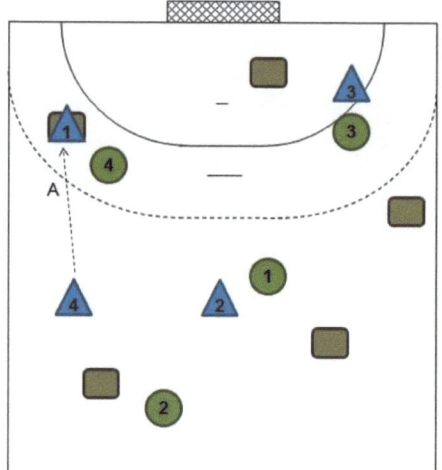

Course:
- The teams play team ball in the playing field.
- The players get a point, if they manage to play a pass to a teammate standing on a box.

⚠ The players are not allowed to stand on a box for more than 3 seconds.

Exercise/objective:
- The attacking players try to score 10 points. If they succeed, the defending players must do 10 push-ups, for example.

Variants:
- Without dribbling.
- Jump shot passes.
- The players must play a double pass with the player standing on the box (the return pass must be played to the player who played the initial pass). This is more challenging for the player receiving the return pass. After playing the pass, he must get into space immediately in order to get the ball. The game becomes much faster!

⚠ The players must adjust quickly, if the player on the box cannot be played a pass.

⚠ The players must already identify the playing/passing possibilities before they receive a pass → Anticipatory playing.

Competitive games for your everyday handball training
60 exercises for every age group

No. 7		Team ball with 4 targets		8	★
	Equipment required:	1 handball, 4 cones, 2 small vaulting boxes, playing field suitable for number of players			

Setting:
- Put two cone goals and two small vaulting boxes (upside down) on the floor in the corners of the playing field.
- Make two teams.

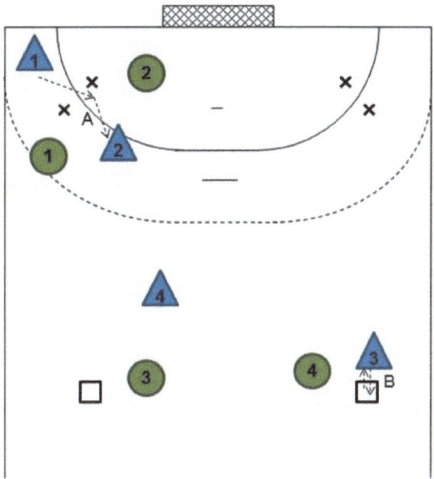

Course:
- The two teams play team ball against each other and try to score points by doing the following:

Either:
- ▲1 plays a bounce pass through the cone goal in such a way that a teammate can catch the ball (A).

Or:
- ▲3 throws the ball into the box in such a way that he can catch it again (B).

Each team defends one cone goal and one box.

Exercise/objective:
- The attacking players try to score 10 points. If they succeed, the defending players must do a predefined exercise.
- The players must adjust quickly, if a target is covered by an opponent.

Variants:
- Allow dribbling.
- No return passes allowed (for larger groups).
- Jump shot passes.
- Passing with the non-throwing hand.
- Do not assign the targets; the players can score points randomly.
- The players can only score a point, if they hit both "targets" (cone and box) one after another.

No. 8	Power team ball	8	★
Equipment required:	8 cones, two playing fields suitable for number of players		

Setting:
- Define two playing fields of similar size with cones.
- Make two teams.

Course:
- Two teams play team ball against each other in the confined playing field (**field 1**), observing the following rules:
    o Each player (**1**, **2**, **3**, and **4**) must have held the ball once and there must have been at least six ball contacts, for example (A).
    o Afterwards, the player must lay down the ball behind the line of cones in the opposite field (**2**) (B).
    o Now, there is a switch in ball possession. **1**, **2**, **3**, and **4** do the same exercise in **field 2** in order to lay down the ball behind the line of cones in **field 1**.
    o If players manage to steal the ball, they start the course in the field in which they stole the ball.

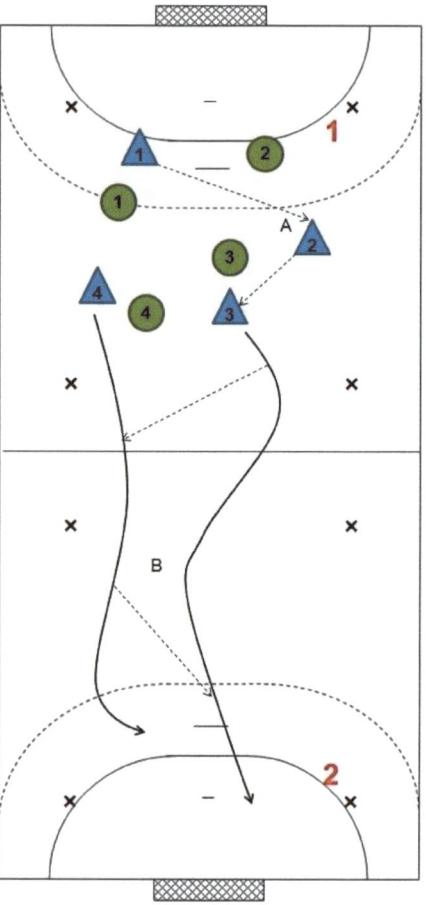

Variant:
- Allow dribbling.

⚠ Quick adjusting leads to a highly dynamic game.

⚠ All players must run at high speed to succeed (laying down/stealing the ball).

No. 9	Team ball on four side lines	12	★★
Equipment required:	1 handball, ½ playing field		

Setting:
- Make 4 teams of at least 3 players.

Course:
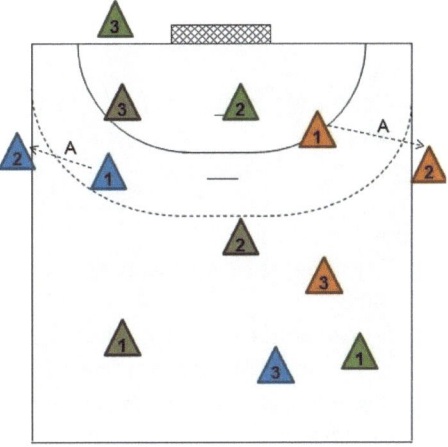
- The teams play team ball against each other.
- The players play towards one of the side lines; they score points by laying down the ball behind the line (A).
- Which team will play towards which side line will be figured out during the game.
- The players who manage to lay down the ball behind a free line "own" this line throughout the whole game.
- The players who laid down the ball must leave the ball there immediately for the other teams.
- A player of another team may now pick up the ball and start playing towards his team's line.
- Dribbling is allowed.

Exercise/objective:
- The players must adjust quickly and fetch the ball swiftly in order to succeed again with their team. The individual tasks change permanently.

Variants:
- Jump shot passes.
- Passing with the non-throwing hand.

Competitive games for your everyday handball training
60 exercises for every age group

No. 10	Team ball with subsequent action	10	★★
Equipment required:	8 cones, 1 handball		

Setting:
- Use cones to define several cone goals.
- Assign the numbers 1 to 4 to the side lines.
- Make two teams.

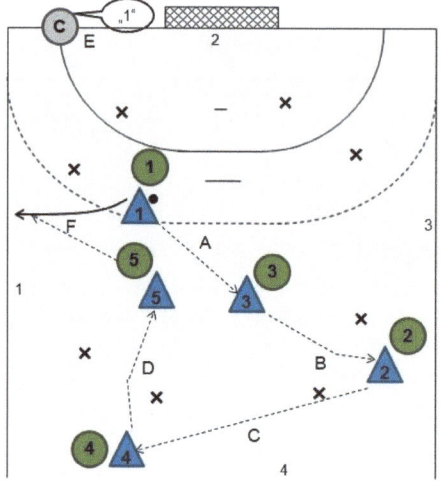

Course:
- The teams play against each other.
- By running and passing the ball in a well-coordinated manner (A), the team in ball possession tries to pass the ball 5 (7) times to a teammate by bouncing it through one of the cone goals (B or D).
- The players must attack a different cone goal each time (C). They are not allowed to bounce the ball through the same cone goal two times in a row.
- The attacking team counts the passes through the cone goals aloud.
- As soon as the players have passed the ball through the cones 5 (7) times, the coach calls out a number between 1 and 4 (E).
- The attacking team now tries to lay down the ball behind the respective side line (F).
- The team scores if they manage to complete the whole course (play five passes through a cone goal and subsequently lay down the ball behind the correct side line).
- The other team fetches the ball and now tries to score a point as well.
- If there is a switch in ball possession, the goal counting starts over from 1.

⚠ The players must adjust quickly and run to the next cone goal immediately after scoring. As soon as the team has played five passes through the cone goals, the players must run to the respective side line immediately.

⚠ Once the scoring team has laid down the ball behind the side line, the other team must fetch the ball immediately and start an attack on the cone goals.

No. 11	Team ball with two different exercises	12	★★
Equipment required:	8 small gym mats, 4 cones, 1 handball		

Setting:
- Define a playing field with the cones and put small gym mats outside the playing field.
- Make two teams.

Course:
- Both teams play team ball within the defined playing field (cones); however, they are not allowed to dribble. If a team manages to pass 8 times in a row, without the other team stealing the ball, the second part of the game begins.
- The attacking players now try to pass the ball to a teammate standing on one of the gym mats (C). If the player on the mat catches the ball, the team scores and stays in possession of the ball. In order to score again however, the team must attack a different gym mat.
- The team does not score if there is an opponent standing on the same gym mat as the attacking player while this player catches the ball (A).
- The players keep playing until the ball is lost.
- The teammates count the score (times they caught the ball while standing on a gym mat) themselves.
- Which team manages to catch the ball on the gym mat most often and scores highest?

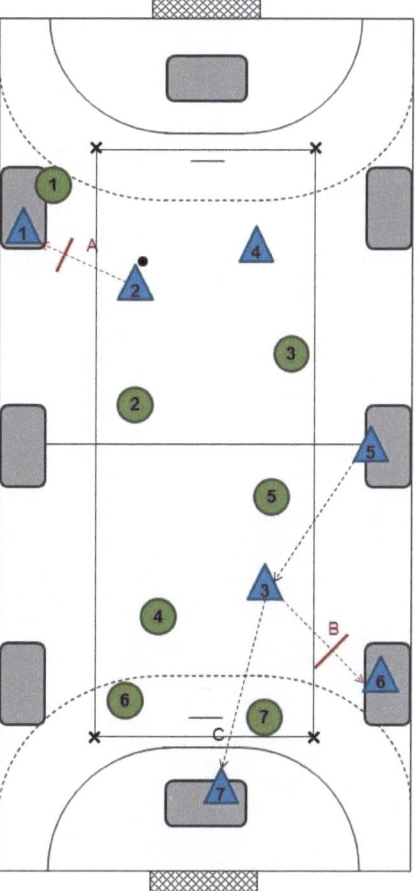

Variants:
- Only a maximum of 3 players per team are allowed in the outer playing field (around the gym mats).
- After scoring, the players are neither allowed to attack the same gym mat again nor to attack the neighboring mats (B).

No. 12	Team ball with subsequent exercise	16	★★
Equipment required:	2 basketball baskets, 3 cones, 1 handball, whistle		

Setting:
- Use cones to divide the upper half of the playing field into two smaller fields.
- Make two teams.
- Divide the two teams in half. The teams play against each other on one quarter of the court (▲1, ▲2, ▲3, and ▲4 play against ●1, ●2, ●3, and ●4 in one quarter, ▲5, ▲6, ▲7, and ▲8 play against ●5, ●6, ●7, and ●8 in the other quarter).

Course:
- The teams play team ball against each other, without dribbling however (A).
- The game starts 4-on-4 in one quarter of the court.
- The players of both teams are not allowed to leave their quarter of the court. However, the ball may be passed into another quarter (B); if this happens, the players keep playing in the other quarter.
- The team in ball possession tries to pass the ball 8 times without interruption.
- Ⓒ has the opportunity to whistle between the 5th and 7th ball contact (C). This is the sign to start the subsequent action. If Ⓒ does not whistle, the players must start the subsequent action automatically after the 8th pass.

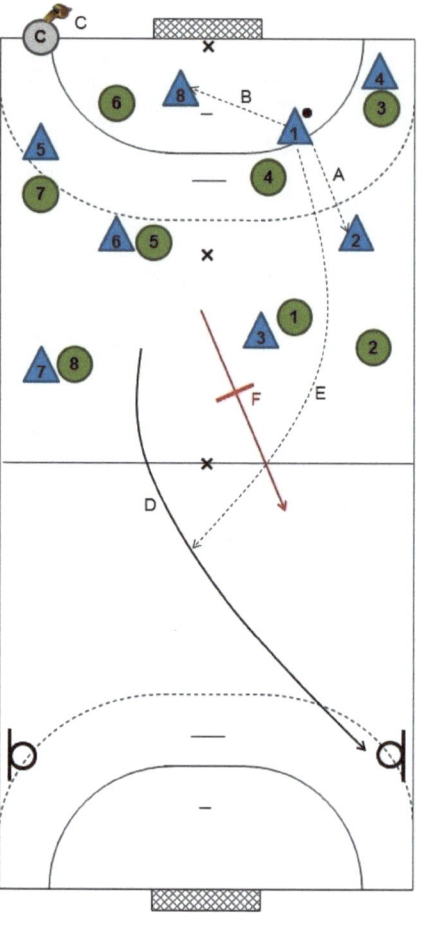

Subsequent action:
- The four players standing in the other quarter (the quarter without ball) once the 8th pass is being played immediately start (D), receive a pass (E), and try to score a point at the diagonal basketball basket. If they succeed, they get a point. However, each player must run around the cone on the center line; they must not run across the other field (F).
- If the defending team manages to win the ball, the course starts over: ①-⑧ try to play 8 passes and may then try to hit the basket.

No. 13	Team ball with change of playing field	8	★★
Equipment required:	8 cones, 3 different types of balls (medicine ball, handball, soft ball, ...)		

Setting:
- Define three playing fields using cones and make two teams.
- Choose a different throwing toy for each playing field, e.g., common handball, medicine ball, frisbee, soft ball, tennis ball, etc.
- After playing, the throwing toys must remain in the respective playing field.

Course:
- Both teams play team ball on the individual playing fields using the respective throwing toy. The players are not allowed to bounce the toy.
- The team in possession of the toy tries to pass it eight times (return passes are not allowed).
- If the opposing team steals the toy, they may immediately try to pass it eight times themselves.
- The team scores, if they manage to pass the toy eight times. After scoring, the toy must be put on the floor at once.

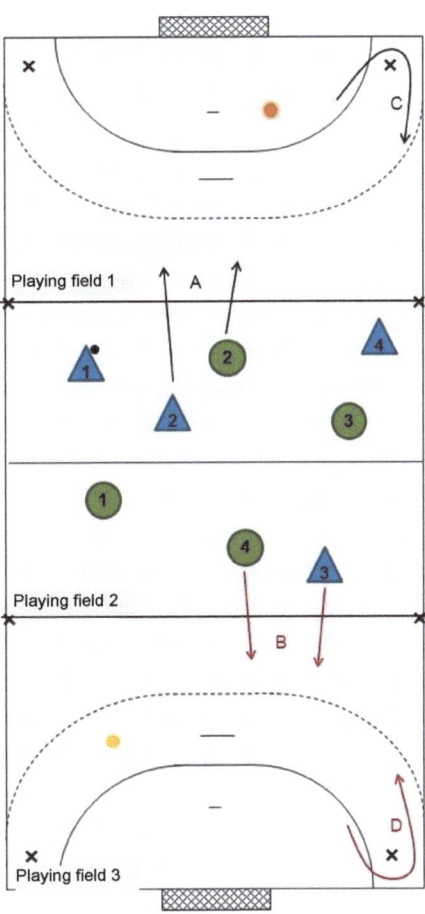

- Now, the coach whistles once or twice, which is the sign for both teams to change the playing field accordingly.

Changing the playing field upon the coach's whistle:
- One whistle: Change playing field upwards (A).
- Two whistles: Change playing field downwards (B).
- The team that first secures the toy may immediately try to pass it 8 times.

Examples:
- End of game on playing field 1
  - One whistle; the players move to playing field 3. However, the players must sprint around one of the two cones first before they are allowed to enter playing field 3 (C).
  - Two whistles; the players move to playing field 2.
- End of game on playing field 2
  - One whistle; the players move to playing field 1.
  - Two whistles; the players move to playing field 3.
- End of game on playing field 3
  - One whistle; the players move to playing field 2.
  - Two whistles; the players move to playing field 3. However, the players must sprint around one of the two cones first before they are allowed to enter playing field 1 (D).

⚠ If the teams remain in one playing field for too long, due to constantly switching ball possession, the coach may whistle anytime in between. The players need to adjust to the new situation repeatedly.

Competitive games for your everyday handball training
60 exercises for every age group

No. 14	Team ball with fast break	9	★★
Equipment required:	1 handball		

Course:

- Make two teams. Both teams play team ball inside the 9-meter zone.
- The attacking team tries to play 10 passes in a row, while trying to keep the players of the defending team from stealing the ball.
- If the defending team steals the ball, the teams switch tasks.
- The goalkeeper always plays in the attacking team and may receive the ball from the players of both teams.
- If the attacking players manage to play 10 passes in a row, they play a pass to the goalkeeper (A) and run a fast break.
- The goalkeeper initiates the fast break by passing the ball to one of the attacking players (B).
- The attacking team scores a point, if they manage to lay down the ball in the opposite 6-meter zone (C).
- The defending players must not block the pass to the goalkeeper. They try to interrupt the fast break so that the attacking team cannot lay down the ball in the opposite 6-meter zone.
- Afterwards, the players do the same course on the other side.

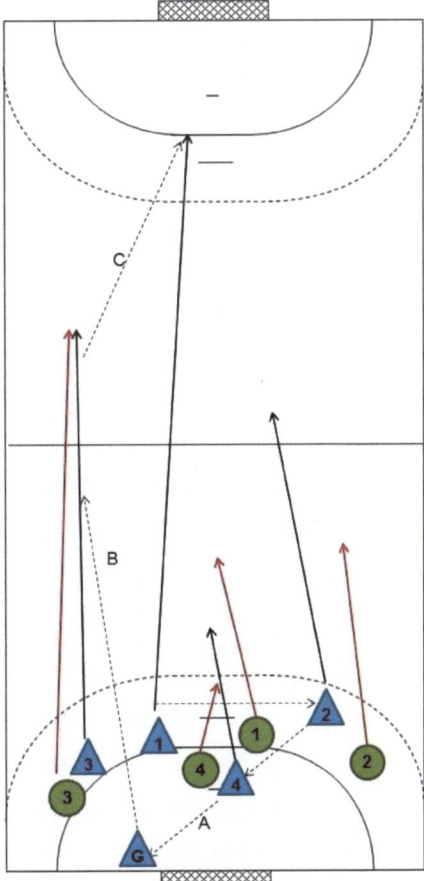

Variants:

- Additional fast break exercises, e.g., the players only score a point, if one of them catches the ball while sitting behind the 6-meter line (or if a player catches the ball and plays a pass to one of his teammates while sitting behind the 6-meter line).

No. 15	Team ball with cone goals and team exercise	8	★★
Equipment required:	8 cones, bibs with tape letters, 2 balance benches, 1 handball		

Preparation:
- Prepare bibs for each team by putting different tape letters on the front and back (see list below).

Setting:
- Put cone goals on the floor of the playing field.
- Put a balance bench on each side of the playing field and allocate the benches to the teams.

Course:
- The teams play in the field, while the players in ball possession try to play a pass to a teammate (A) in such a way that he can play a bounce pass to another teammate (B). The team has scored then.
- If the players manage to play a pass through a cone goal, they keep on playing (C); they must score their next point at another cone goal however.
- The defending team tries to steal the ball and score points themselves.
- Upon the coach's whistle (after about 2 minutes), both teams sprint back to their bench (D) and stand on the bench.
- The coach then says a word which the players must form, with the letters on their bibs as fast as they can (and which can be read from the coach's point of view). However, the players are not allowed to leave the bench (they must be able to pass each other instead).
- The team who first manages to form the word gets 5 points.
- Afterwards, the teams start attacking the cone goals again (ball possession switches).
- Which team scores highest?

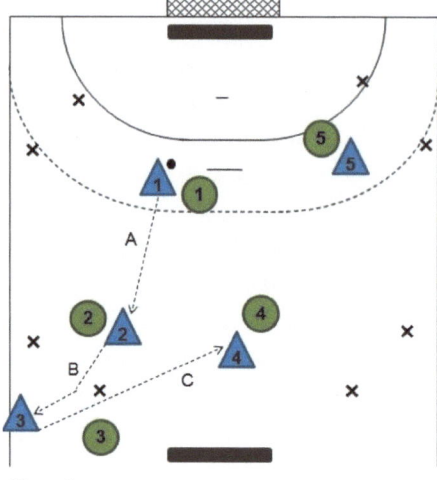

Figure 1

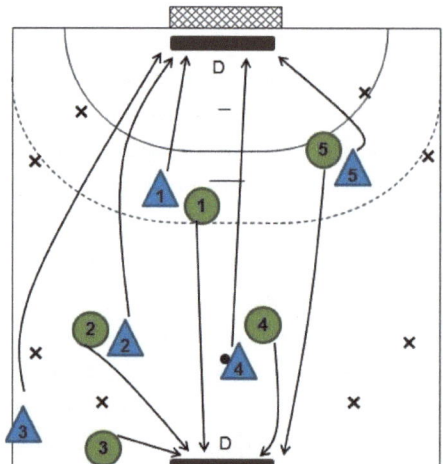

Figure 2

Example 1: Possible letter combinations:
- **4 players** per team (front/back): E/M, T/E, H/T, A/S
  Words: Hate, Heat, Mets, Stem
- **5 players** per team: additionally: R/I
  Words: Earth, Hater, Heart, Smite, Items, Times
- **6 players** per team: additionally: S/L
  Words: Earths, Haters, Hearts

Example 2: Possible letter combinations:
- **4 players** per team (front/back): A/O, S/E, N/E, R/S
  Words: Ears, Nose, Ones
- **5 players** per team: additionally: T/R
  Words: Taser, Rates, Snore
- **6 players** per team: additionally: W/D
  Words: Rawest, Waters, Waster, Drones, Snored

No. 16	Team ball with moving 2	8	★★
Equipment required:	Playing field suitable for number of players which is divided into four identical smaller fields (with cones, for example), 1 handball		

Setting:
- Divide the playing field into four smaller fields using cones (I to IV).
- Make two teams.

Course:
- The teams play team ball against each other.
- The player who will receive the pass must not stand in the same field as the player who plays the pass, but in one of the other three fields.
- Without dribbling.

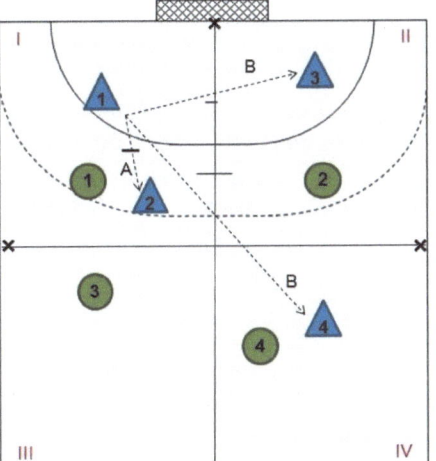

Pass allowed: (B)
Pass not allowed: (A)

Exercise/objective:
- The attacking players try to play 10 passes. If they succeed, the defending players must do a predefined exercise.

Variants:
- No return passes allowed (for larger groups).
- Jump shot passes.
- Passing with the non-throwing hand.

Team play with different targets

No. 17	Bucket ball	8	★
Equipment required:	2 buckets, 2 small gym mats, 1 handball		

Setting:
- Make two teams.
- Put a mat on the floor on each side of the playing field. One player of the respective attacking team stands on the target mat holding a bucket in his hands.

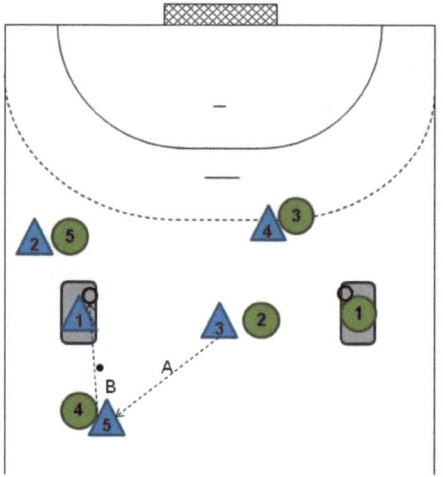

Course:
- The attacking team tries to score a point by playing quick passes (A) and throwing the ball into the bucket (B). The player on the mat may help by catching the ball with the bucket. He may only move on the mat.
- The other players (defense and offense) are not allowed to step on the mat.
- The defending team tries to prevent the attacking team from throwing the ball at the mat.
- Once a point has been scored, ball possession switches and another player stands on the mat.

Variants:
- Without dribbling.
- The game is suitable for other throwing toys as well (small cherry pit cushions or juggling balls).
- Instead of holding a bucket, the player on the mat holds a hoop through which the players must pass the ball.

No. 18	Pyramid ball	6	★
Equipment required:	1 handball pyramid, 1 handball		

Setting:
- Draw a circle on the court floor or use already existing lines.
- Put a handball pyramid into the circle (or use a large vaulting box).

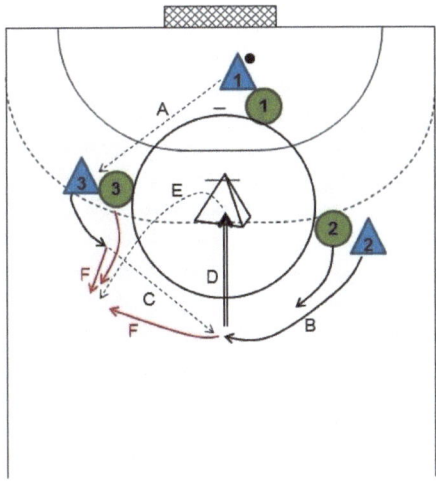

Course:
- Two teams play against each other.
- By passing quickly (A and C) and moving in a well-coordinated manner (B), the team in ball possession tries to put a player in a good position so that he can shoot at the pyramid (D).
- Every time a player hits the pyramid, the team scores a point.
- Both teams may try to win the ball (F) as it bounces back from the pyramid (E). The team who catches the ball is the attacking team and tries to score more points. If the team who just scored catches the ball again, they get an extra point.
- Which team scores highest?

Competitive games for your everyday handball training
60 exercises for every age group

No. 19	Pass to player behind the line	10	★
Equipment required:	4 cones, 1 handball		

Setting:
- Define two existing lines as finish lines with cones.
- Make two teams.

Course:
- Two teams play against each other.
- By playing quick passes (A, B) and moving in a well-coordinated manner (C), the team in ball possession tries to pass to a player in such a way (D) that he can lay down the ball behind the finish line of his team (E). The team has scored then.
- The players are not allowed to dribble.
- Once the ball lies behind the line, the other team fetches it immediately and starts an attack towards the other line.
- Which team scores highest?

⚠ The players should cleverly get into space near the line so that they can lay down the ball immediately after they received the pass.

⚠ The players must catch the ball in front of the line; they must not stand behind the line while catching the ball.

No. 20	Kempa with safety mat	8	★
Equipment required:	2 large safety mats, 1 handball		

Setting:
- Put a large safety mat on the floor on each side of the playing field.
- Make two teams. Each team defends one safety mat.

Course:
- By playing quick passes (A) and moving in a well-coordinated manner, the teams try to pass to a player in such a way (B) that he can catch the ball while jumping onto the mat (C).
- If the player catches the ball in the air and afterwards lands on the mat, the team gets a point.
- A team may try to score several times in a row. If the player does not catch the ball while jumping onto the mat, or if he lands on the mat before catching the ball, the team may keep on playing and try again.
- Once a team has scored, ball possession switches and the other team starts an attack towards the other mat.

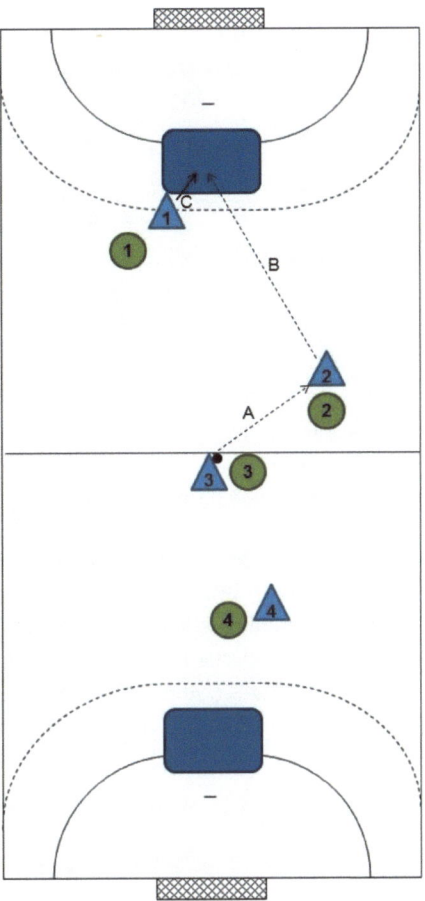

⚠ The players may act around the mat, i.e., also run behind the mat and jump onto it from this position.

No. 21	Playing with 3 vaulting boxes	8	★
Equipment required:	3 large vaulting boxes, 1 handball		

Setting:

- Put three large vaulting boxes on the playing field and allocate them to the teams as their "goals".
- 🔺1, 🔺2, 🔺3, and 🔺4 attack "B" and defend "C".
- 🔵1, 🔵2, 🔵3, and 🔵4 attack "C" and defend "B".
- Box "A" serves as goal for both teams.
- In order to score (goal), the players must hit the front/back of the box.
- The game is to be played observing team handball rules.

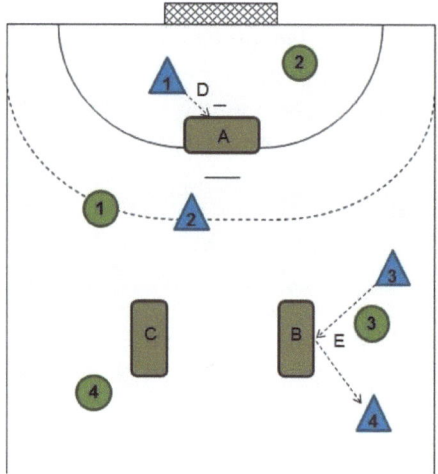

Course:

- The team in ball possession gets a point if they manage to throw the ball at the respective surface of the box (D). However, the player who threw the shot is not allowed to pick up the ball right afterwards.
- If a teammate catches the ball after the shot at the box (E), the team stays in ball possession and may keep on trying to score.

Variant:

- Each vaulting box may serve as a goal.
- The vaulting box which was last attacked must not be attacked again right afterwards. The players must try to attack another box first.

No. 22	Touch ball with safety mat	8	★★
Equipment required:	2 large safety mats, 1 handball		

Setting:
- Put a large safety mat on the floor on each side of the playing field.
- Make two teams.

Course:
- Each team tries to lay down the ball on their opponents' gym mats.
- If a defending player ⑤ touches the attacking player who has the ball ▲3, the attacking player is allowed to play backward passes only. If he plays a forward pass, ball possession switches.

⚠ The defending players should immediately run towards the attacking player who has the ball and try to touch him.

⚠ Even before they get the ball, the attacking players should analyze which teammate is in the closest and best position so that they can pass the ball immediately.

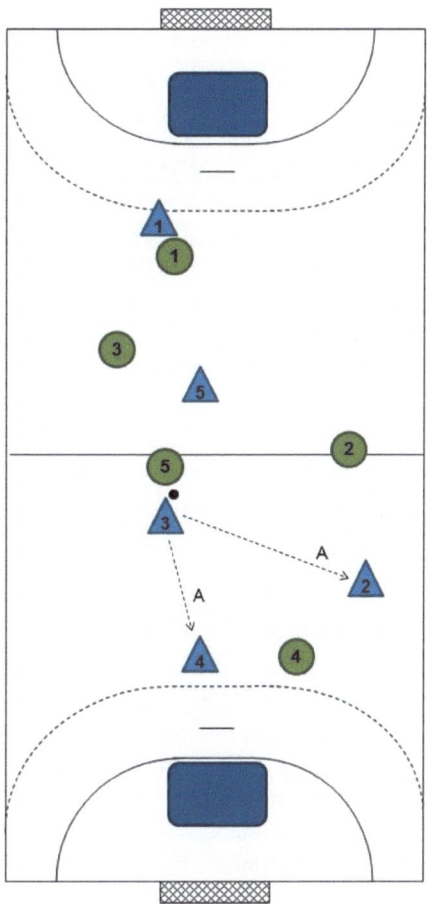

⚠ For a small group, dribbling is not allowed. In this way, the speed of the game increases significantly, as the players must get into space over and over again.

Competitive games for your everyday handball training
60 exercises for every age group

No. 23	Diagonal team ball in 4 teams	10	★★
Equipment required:	4 small gym mats, 1 handball		

Setting:
- Put four small gym mats into the corners of the playing field.
- Make 2 teams; each team consists of 2 sub-teams (in the example: if you have 5 players per team, divide them into a sub-team of 2 and a sub-team of 3).

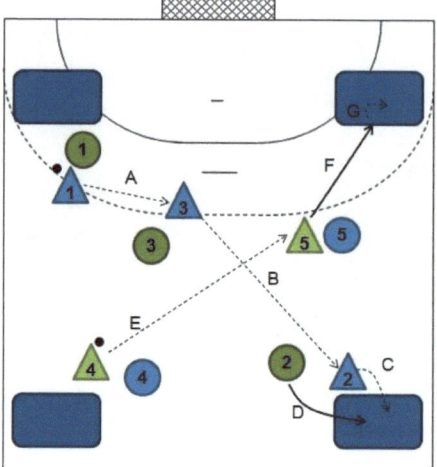

Overall course:
- The two sub-teams of 3 play against each other on a playing field between two mats diagonal to each other. The two sub-teams of 2 play against each other on the playing field between the other mats diagonal to each other.
- At the end, the points of both sub-teams are added; this is the total score of the whole team.
- Which team scores highest?

Course:
- By playing quick passes (A, B, and E), the team in ball possession tries to position a player next to the opponents' mat so that he can be passed to and lay the ball on the mat (C and G). The team has scored then.
- Once the ball is on the mat, the defending team secures the ball (D) and starts a counter attack on the opponents' mat.
- When playing 2-on-2, the players may dribble (F).

⚠ Since the teams play 3-on-3 and 2-on-2 on diagonal playing fields at the same time, the players must keep in mind that there will be some traffic when playing the individual actions. The players must approach the opponents' mat, but also pay attention to the other teams crossing their field diagonally.

⚠ If there are more players or fewer players per team, split the teams accordingly (2 times 3-on-3; 2 times 2-on-2).

No. 24	**Laying down the ball and bridging playing fields**	10	★★
Equipment required:	1 ball, cones as needed to define the playing field		

Setting:
- Define a field for the goalkeeper in the center of the playing field (use lines or cones).
- Make two teams. Both teams play team ball against each other.

Throwing toy:
- Choose a ball which does either not bounce ("catchball") or is hard to control during dribbling ("unball").

Course:
- The team in ball possession tries to lay down the ball in the opposite 6-meter zone (A, C, E, F, and G).
- The player who is about to lay down the ball must catch it outside of the 6-meter zone before laying it down on the floor (G).
- T may receive a pass from the players of the team in ball possession at any time. He may move freely in his field (B). The field players are not allowed to step into the goalkeeper's field however.
- The players **must** pass the ball to T every time they cross the center line (C and E or F).
- The players must not cross the center line while holding the ball (D).
- Every time the players manage to lay down the ball, they score a point. Subsequently, the players of the other team may pick up the ball at once and try to lay it down in the opposite 6-meter zone to score a point. The players of the other team must pass the ball to T when crossing the center line as well. And so on.
- Define an exercise for the loser team before the game.

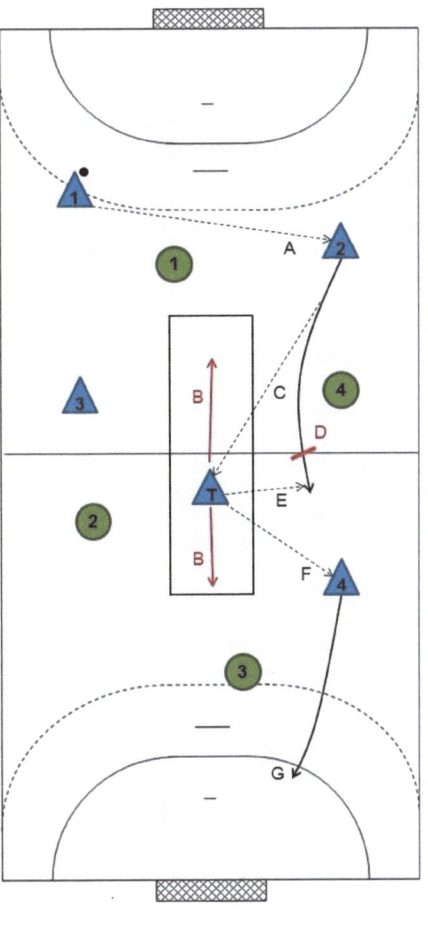

No. 25	3:2-outnumbered competition	12	★★
Equipment required:	3 ball boxes, 10 or more handballs, 4 cones, playing field suitable for number of players		

Setting:
- Define a suitable playing field with cones.
- Put a ball box containing handballs on the floor, an empty ball box on the opposite, and a third ball box on the side for the defending players.

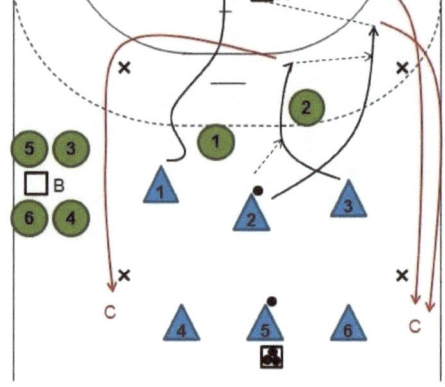

Course:
- 1, 2, and 3 play against 1 and 2 and try to lay the ball into their box (A).
- After each attack, the players must run around the cones and back as fast as they can (C).
- Afterwards, the next group starts (4, 5, and 6) with a ball.
- 1 and 2 also run back to their group and the next two players (3 and 4) start.
- If the two defending players manage to win the ball or to block an attacking player holding the ball for three seconds so that he cannot play a pass anymore, the defending players win the ball and lay it into their own ball box (B). Afterwards, it is the next defending players' turn. The attacking players must run around the cones first (C) before the new attacking players are allowed to start.
- Repeat the course until there are no balls left in the ball box. Afterwards, the players switch roles and the entire course starts over. Which team has the most balls in their box?

⚠ The game may be played with fewer players, too. The game intensifies significantly: If there are four players per team, for example (5, 6; 5, 6 are taken out), two players must start over immediately every time to play the next attack 3-on-2 with the remaining players.

No. 26	Dice ball with additional exercise	10	★★
Equipment required:	Foam dice, small vaulting box, 1 handball		

Setting:
- Make two teams.
- Draw a circle in the center of the court floor or use an already existing circle.
- Put a small vaulting box inside the circle and put a foam dice on top.

Course of action 1:
- One team (1, 2, 3, 4, and 5) starts as attacking team. By playing quick passes (A and B), the attacking players try to get into a good shooting position in order to hit the dice on the box (C).
- The other team tries to prevent the attacking team from shooting at the dice; they try to win the ball.
- If they win the ball, the defending team may try to hit the dice on the box themselves.
- The team which hits the dice gets a point.
- Immediately after a team has scored, action 2 starts.

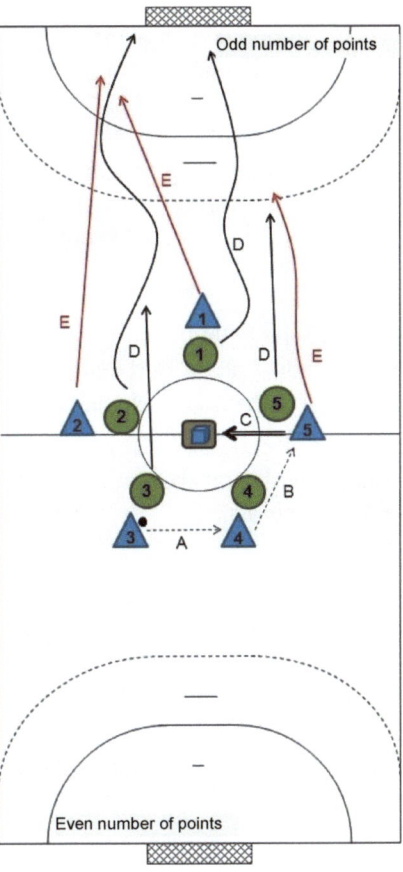

Course of action 2:
- Once the dice has been hit, both teams try to secure the ball.
- The number of points on the dice indicates towards which side line the teams play afterwards:
    - If the number of points is odd (1, 3, or 5), the teams play towards the upper side line (as shown in the figure).
    - If the number of points is even (2, 4, or 6), the teams play towards the lower side line.
- The team which won the ball, tries to lay down the ball behind the respective side line as fast as possible (D). If the players succeed, they get a point.
- The other players become the defending team and try to prevent the attacking players from scoring a point (E).

Overall course:
- Count the teams' points scored at the box and at the side line.
- The teams attack and defend alternately in the beginning.
- Which team scores highest after 20 rounds?

⚠ After the shot at the small box, the players must swiftly secure the ball and start the second action.

Competitive games for your everyday handball training
60 exercises for every age group

Tag games

No. 27	**Tag rally**	6 (12)	★
Equipment required:	6 cones, two playing fields suitable for number of players		

Course:

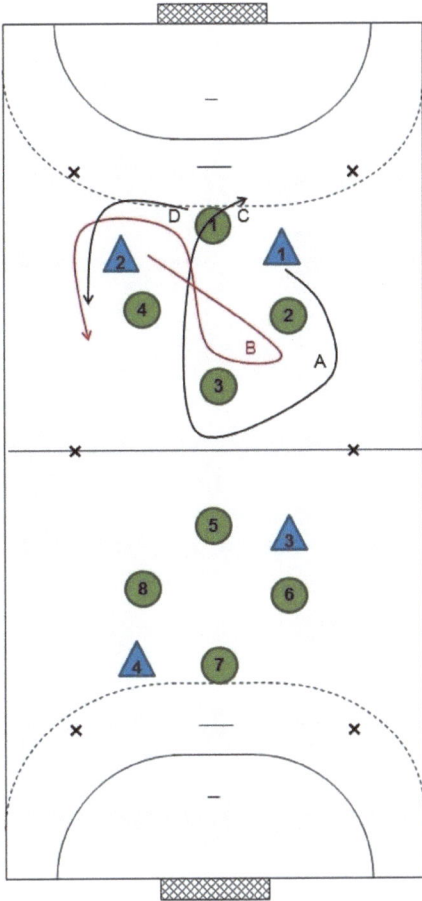

- The players spread out on the two playing fields, as shown in the example with six players per field.
- ①, ②, ③, and ④ lie down on the floor face down (forming a star; heads towards the center).
- ② is the catcher (B).
- ① takes quick turns and tries to prevent ② from catching him (A).
- If, for example, ① jumps over ①, who lies on the floor (C), ① becomes the new catcher and must try to catch ② (D). ① lies down on the floor in ①'s former position.
- If a catcher (②) manages to catch the fleeing player (①) before he has jumped over another player (①, for example), the players switch roles and the former fleeing player becomes the catcher.
- The group in the other field does the same course.

⚠ The groups should not be too large, otherwise the players will have to wait for too long until it is their turn.

⚠ Request immediate adjusting to the lying, catching, and fleeing situations (short reaction time, permanent change of tasks).

No. 28	Team tag on two fields	10	★
Equipment required:			

Basic setting:
- Make 2 teams.
- The center line is the "boundary" of the playing field.

Course:
- On command, one player per team (1 and 1) starts to run, crosses the center line (A), and tries to tag a player of the other team (B).
- If 1 succeeds (C), he immediately runs back and crosses the center line. The team has scored then. Now, another player of the same team (3) is allowed to cross the center line in order to tag a player of the other team as fast as possible (D).

Tasks:
- Which team scores highest within 2 minutes?
- Each player of a team must tag two times (between the two "taggings", he must run back and cross the center line).

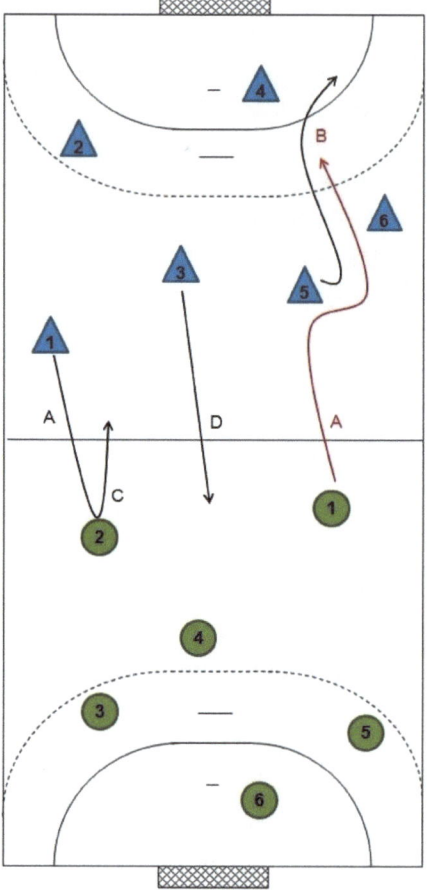

⚠ Only one player per team is allowed to cross the center line. If two players of the same team have crossed the center line, the team does not score, even though one of them may have tagged an opponent!

⚠ If 1 is in the "opponents'" half and is about to tag a player, he may not be tagged by 1. Players may only be tagged if they are in their own half of the playing field (and not in the opponents' half).

No. 29	Sprint competition with playing cards	6	★
Equipment required:	1 large vaulting box, 1 game of cards		

Setting:
- Put the vaulting box in the center of the playing field.
- The players stand in two lines at the upper and lower edge of the large vaulting box.
- Take the cards and make two piles (the left pile is for the players belonging to ①, the right pile is for the players belonging to ②). Put the piles in front of you.

Course:
- Flip one card of each pile.
- The player with the higher card becomes the catcher (A).
- The player with the lower card must try to run into the 6-meter zone of his part of the playing field without being touched by the catcher (B).
- If the catcher touches him, the fleeing player must do push-ups/sit-ups, for example.

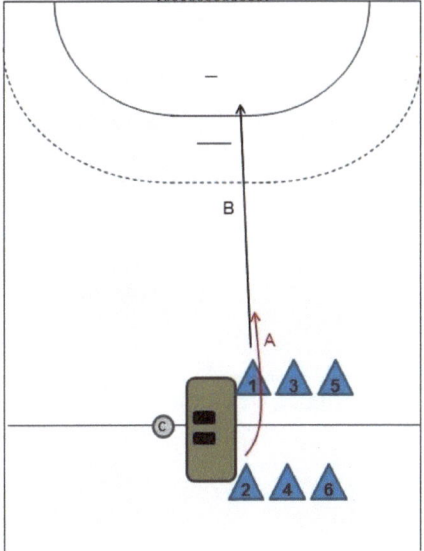

⚠ Make new pairs after each round.

⚠ The distance between the two players must be large enough so that they cannot touch/hit each other while standing.

No. 30	Chasing competition	6	★
Equipment required:	2 cones		

Setting:
- Define a start line with cones.
- The teams make groups of 2.

Course:
- The attacking player  runs towards his teammate ① on the other side.
- ① stands on the other side at a distance of about 10-15 meters and stretches out his hand. ▲ runs to ① and hits his hand (A); this is the sign to start. ① now tries to catch/touch the attacking player ▲ (B) before crossing his start line again.

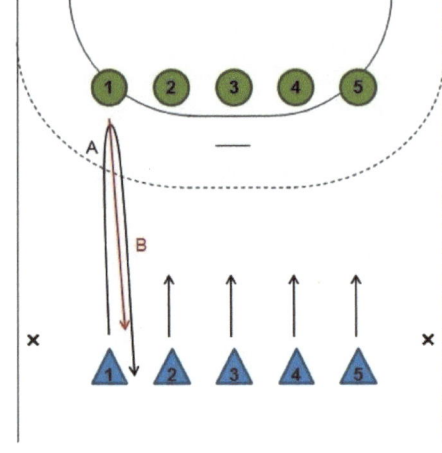

⚠ The attacking players should change their speed when running towards the other player or delay/vary the time they hit the hand.

Competitive games for your everyday handball training
60 exercises for every age group

No. 31	Rope tag	8	★
Equipment required:	One skipping rope per player		

Setting:
- Each player has a skipping rope which he folds once or twice and then puts it in the back of his shorts in such a way that at least 20 to 30 centimeters of the rope hang out.
- Define a suitable field according to the number of players.

Course:
- The players crisscross.
- While doing this, they try to steal the other players' ropes (A).
- If a player manages to steal the rope from another player (B), he puts this rope in his shorts as well and then keeps on running with the two ropes (C).
- The player who does not have a rope anymore now tries to steal one (D).
- The coach whistles after 2 minutes. The player who has the most ropes gets a point.
- Who has scored highest after 4 rounds?

No. 32	"Ball holding means safe" play tag	9	★★
Equipment required:	2 handballs		

Course:
- Two players try to catch the other players (A).
- The player who is holding the ball and the player who held the ball last must not be caught.
- Hence, the fleeing players always must pass the ball to the player who is currently in danger of being caught (B).
- Once a player has been caught, he becomes the catcher.

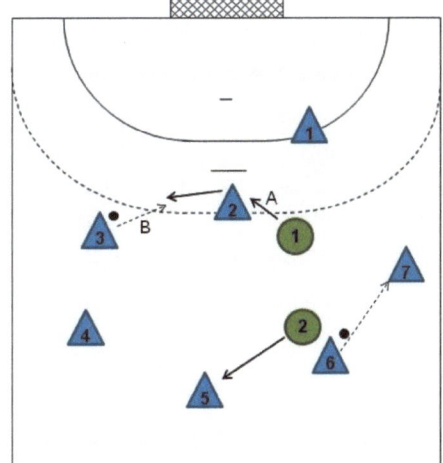

⚠ There must be as much balls in the game as there are catchers.

⚠ Tag the catchers (let them carry a bib, for example).

No. 33	Play tag with ball	8	★★
Equipment required:	4 cones, 1 handball		

Setting:
- Define a suitable playing field with 4 cones.
- In the beginning, 2 players are catchers. Tag the other players (let them carry a bib, for example).

Course:
- The players spread out on the field.
- The two catchers (in the figure, ① and ②) pass a ball (A).
- While doing this, they try to catch the other players. The player holding the ball must touch them with his other hand (B).
- Only the player holding the ball is allowed to catch a player (B). He is allowed to make three steps at the most; he is not allowed to dribble.
- The catcher not holding the ball is not allowed to catch; he must move in a well-coordinated manner so that he is in a good position to touch another player once he gets the ball (C).
- A player who has been touched becomes an extra catcher.
- The players keep playing until all the players have been caught. Then, two new players become catchers.

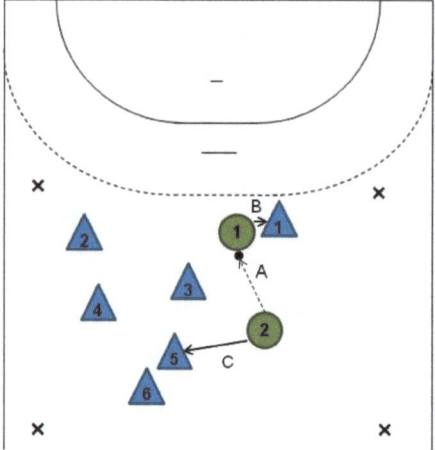

⚠ The fleeing players should not steal the ball, but try to avoid being caught by moving in a well-coordinated manner.

⚠ Make the task easier for the catchers by choosing a smaller field or a larger number of catchers in the beginning.

No. 34	1-on-1 play tag	6	★★
Equipment required: 6 cones			

Setting:
- Define the starting positions and the finish lines as well as a goal in the center with cones.

Course:
- 1 and 4 start on command.
- 1 tries to cross the opposite line without being touched by 4 (A).
- 4 tries to catch 1 and tag him (B).
- If 1 manages to cross the line without being touched, he gets a point. If 4 touches him before, 4 gets a point.
- Afterwards, 2 and 5 start the same course. Keep going until all the players of the team have done the exercise. Switch tasks afterwards.
- Which team scores highest? The losing team must do push-ups or sit-ups.

Variant:
- If 1 crosses the line directly (A), he gets one point. If 1 takes the longer way through the cone goal and then crosses the line without being touched, he gets two points (C).

Sprint and relay race games

No. 35	Game of pairs with sprint	6	★
Equipment required:	1 large vaulting box, 2 cones, 1 game of pairs		

Setting:
- Put a large vaulting box near the center line and put the game of pairs face-down on top.

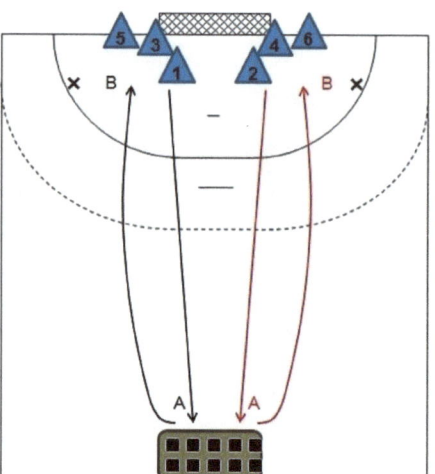

Course:
- On command, 1 and 2 start simultaneously. They run to the vaulting box and flip two cards each, memorize the pictures, and flip them again.
- Afterwards, the two players run back and exchange a high-five with the next player who then flips two cards as well.
- If a player flips a matching pair (two identical cards), he takes the cards along to his teammates.
- The players repeat the course until there are no more cards left on the box.

Objective:
- The team who has found the most pairs wins.

⚠ The players should discuss the positions of the cards so that they find the matching pairs faster.

Variant:
- Each team gets their own game of pairs on a small vaulting box.

The losing team must do push-ups or sit-ups ...

No. 36	Sprint course with playing cards	6	★
Equipment required:	2 balance benches, 4 small vaulting boxes, 3 small gym mats, 1 large vaulting box, 1 game of cards, 4 cones		

Setting:
- Define the running path with 4 cones.
- Put the cards face-down on top of the large vaulting box at the center line.
- Position 2 balance benches on the floor in a row (C).
- Put 4 small vaulting boxes on the floor (D).
- Position 3 small gym mats (E).
- Leave sufficient space between the equipment.

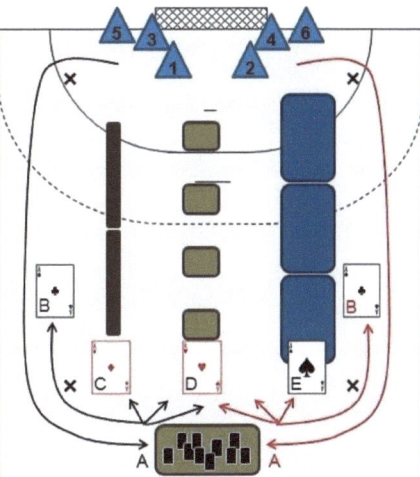

Course:
- On command, 1 and 2 simultaneously start to run around the cones and towards the vaulting box (A) where they flip a card.
- They take the card with them and do the following exercise, depending on the card suit:
    - **Diamonds (C):** The player must lie face-down on the first balance bench and pull himself forward over the first bench using both hands. Then he must get up and jump over the 2nd balance bench, always from the right to the left (he must do at least 4 jumps).
    - **Hearts (D):** The player must jump on the small vaulting box with both legs, jump down again, and jump on the next box.
    - **Spades (E):** The player must do 3 somersaults on the gym mats.
    - **Clubs (B):** The player must run back around the cones on the outer side.
- Afterwards, the player must exchange a high-five with the next player who then does the same course.
- Which team is the fastest?

Repetition:
- Each player must run 3 times.

Variants:
- In the beginning, each team draws 20 cards, for example, from the pile. The teammates distribute the cards among themselves. Each player runs to the box with a card and then does the exercise defined by the card suit on the way back.

The losing team must do push-ups, sit-ups, ...

No. 37	Medicine ball relay race	3	★
Equipment required:	One medicine ball per group of three		

Setting:
- Make teams of 3; each team gets a medicine ball (as shown in the figure).
- The players each stand next to the side line.

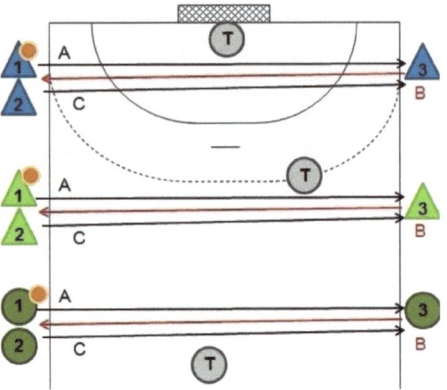

Course:
- On command, the players start with the medicine ball (🔺1, 🔺1, and 🔵1), sprint to the other side, and, once they reach the level of the side line, hand over the medicine ball to the next player (A).
- 🔺3, 🔺3, and 🔵3 sprint to the other side while holding the medicine ball (B) and, once they reach the level of the side line, hand over the medicine ball to the next player.
- 🔺2, 🔺2, and 🔵2 sprint to the other side while holding the medicine ball (C) and, once they reach the level of the side line, hand over the medicine ball to the first player again.
- Repeat the drill 30 (60) times in total. The team who is then first to cross the side line with the medicine ball wins.

Define exercises beforehand:
- The winner does not have to do an exercise.
- The 2nd must do 10 quick jumping jacks, for example.
- The 3rd must do 10 push-ups, for example.
- And so on.

⚠ Make sure the players hand over the medicine ball correctly once they reach the level of the side line. The players must not start too early or pass the ball.

⚠ Add a "counting player" to each group (C) who counts the number of rounds.

No. 38	"Going to Jerusalem" rope skipping	6	⭐
Equipment required:	One skipping rope per player, foam beams (1 beam less than there are players)		

Setting:
- Each player takes a skipping rope.
- Spread out the foam beams across the court (see figure).
- Spread 2 to 3 beams less than there are players.

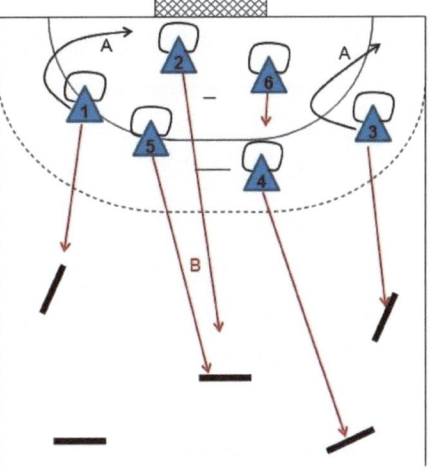

Course 1:
- The players crisscross across the 9-meter zone while skipping (A).
- On command, the players stop skipping and sprint to one of the beams on the floor (B):
    o They should take the rope along.
    o The player who first has his foot on the beam, owns that beam.
- The players who do not own a beam, must do an exercise (10 quick jumping jacks, 5 push-ups, for example).
- Afterwards, the players come back and start over again.

Course 2:
- Use 1 beam less than there are players (example: 10 players → 9 beams).
- The players crisscross again across the 9-meter zone while skipping (A).
- On command, the players stop skipping and sprint to one of the beams on the floor (B).
- The player who does not get a beam is disqualified and must do 10 push-ups and 10 sit-ups on the side, for example.
- Afterwards, remove one beam. The remaining players start the course over in the 9-meter zone (9 players → 8 beams).
- Repeat the course until only two players are left. They are the winners.

⚠️ Players who leave the 9-meter zone before the command disqualify and must do the predefined exercise.

No. 39	Collecting playing cards and throwing at the basket	6	★
Equipment required:	1 game of cards, 1 large vaulting box, 2 basketball baskets, one handball per group, 2 cones		

Setting:
- Make teams of 2 or 3 players and allocate them a card (Jacks, 7s, Kings, for example).
- Spread out the cards face-down on top of the box.

Course:
- On command, the first players of each group start simultaneously and sprint to the box while holding a ball.
- There, they flip a card. If a player flips one of the allocated cards, he takes it with him, sprints back (A),

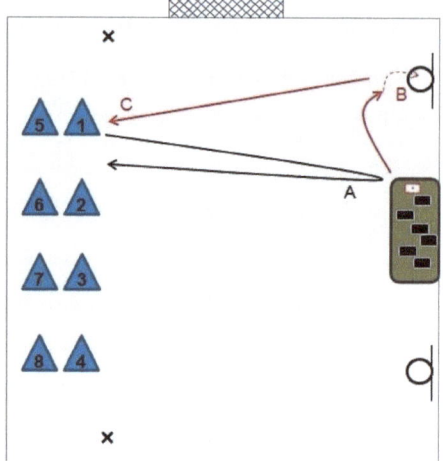

and hands over the ball to the next player (5, for example) who then also sprints to the box. The players keep going until all 4 cards have been collected.
- If he flips a wrong card, 1 must take a turn towards the basketball basket (after he has flipped the card again and left it on the box) and must throw at the basket until he has scored a point (B).
- Afterwards, 1 runs back and hands over the ball to 5 (C).

The team who has collected all four cards first wins.

No. 40	Corner sprint on command	6	★
Equipment required:	2 small gym mats		

Setting:
- Put two mats in the center of the field, put four cones in the corners and allocate them the numbers 1 to 4 (see figure).
- Make two teams. Each team lines up behind a gym mat.

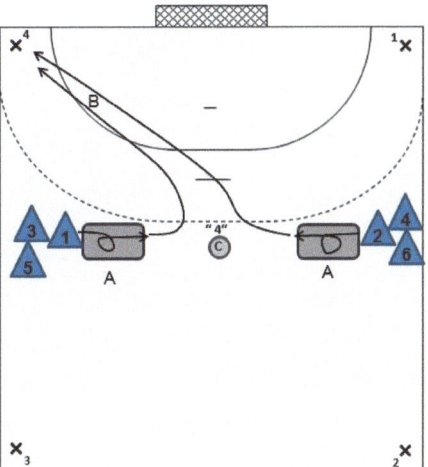

Course:
- On command, 1 and 2 start simultaneously and do a somersault on the mat (A).
- While they do the somersault, the coach calls out a number between 1 and 4 (here "4").
- After the somersault, the players must sprint to the respective corner (B).
- The player who arrives first scores a point for his team.
- On command, the next two players start.

Variants:
- The coach calls out a calculation task instead of a number. The result must be 1, 2, 3, or 4 (21-18, 12/6, root of 16, for example).
- The coach does not call out numbers, but shows colored cards or bibs instead (4 colors). Each corner has been allocated a color.

⚠ The players should orientate towards the correct corner immediately after the somersault.

No. 41	Sprint competition with two groups and different exercises	10	★★
Equipment required:	1 large safety mat, 11 cones, 1 handball		

Setting:
- Put the mat and the cones on the floor as shown in the figure.
- Make two teams.

Course of team 1:
- The players pass the ball from the left wing position to the right wing position (A) and back (D).
- Once 1 has passed the ball to 2, he sprints to the left goal post, touches it, and sprints back again (B).
- Once 2 has passed the ball to 3, he sprints to the left goal post, touches it, and sprints back again.
- Once 3 has passed the ball to 4, he sprints to the large safety mat (C), touches it, and sprints back again.
- 4 passes to 5 who plays a return pass to 4, sprints to the right goal post, touches it, and sprints back again.
- And so on.

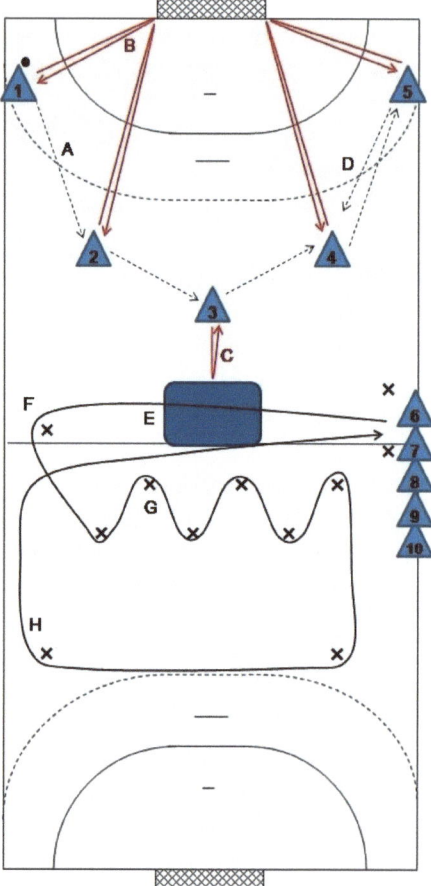

Notes:
- 3 sprints each time.
- 1 and 2 only sprint, if the ball comes from the left side.
- 4 and 5 only sprint, if the ball comes from the right side.

Course of team 2:
- All players start running behind each other to the large safety mat.
- They do 6 steps (3 left and 3 right) on the safety mat (E).

- The players run around the cone behind each other (F) and through the cones in a forward-backward movement.
- Afterwards, they run on a curved path around the cones and cross the start and finish line (H).

Overall course:
- Team 2 does five rounds. Count the number of passes of team 1, afterwards the teams switch tasks.
- Which team has played the most passes?

No. 42	Team pendulum relay race	8	★★
Equipment required:	4 cones		

Setting:
- Position cones as shown in the figure.

Course:
- On command, 1 and 5 start simultaneously and sprint to the cone in the back, run around the cone (A), and sprint back again.
- They take 2 (1) and 6 (5) by the hand (B) and sprint around the cone (A) and back as a pair.
- Afterwards, they take the third player by the hand etc. until all players sprint around the cone hand in hand.
- As soon as the last player has been "picked up", the players run around the cone in the back together (A).
- Once they have come back, 1 and 5 let go and the other players sprint around the cone again (A).
- In each round and in reverse order, one of the players is allowed to let go at the starting position until only one player is left, who then sprints the last round alone.
- The losing team must do push-ups or sit-ups, for example.

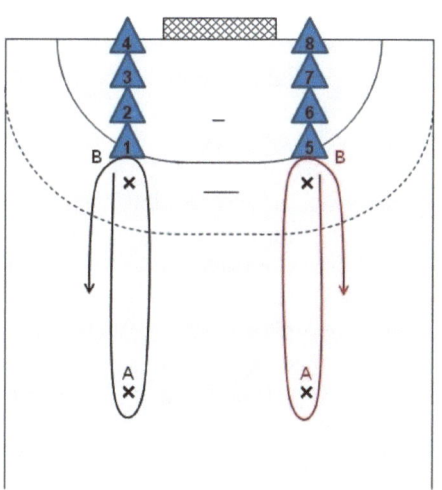

⚠ The competition is quite intense, as each player must sprint several rounds in a row.

⚠ Tactical running might be useful (due to the high physical strain, you cannot predict the winner before the end of the exercise).

Competitive games for your everyday handball training
60 exercises for every age group

No. 43	Sprint relay race with passing	8	★★
Equipment required:	2 handballs		

Setting:
- Make 2 teams with one handball each.
- The players of both teams line up behind the center line.

Course:
- On command, one player per team sprints into the 6-meter zone (A).
- Once he has arrived in the 6-meter zone, he receives a pass (B) and plays a return pass immediately (C).
- As soon as the ball has come back to the center line (D), the players repeat the course and the next player sprints etc.
- Once the last player has the ball, he passes it back to his teammate in the 6-meter zone (F), sprints, steps into the 6-meter zone with one foot, and immediately sprints back to the center line (G).
- As soon as he has arrived, he receives a pass (J) and plays a return pass immediately (K).
- The next player sprints to the center, receives a pass, and passes back into the 6-meter zone.
- Repeat the course until it is the last player's turn. Once he has the ball, he dribbles back and crosses the center line.
- Which team is the fastest?

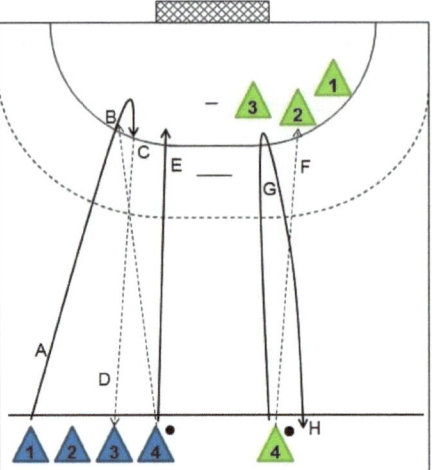

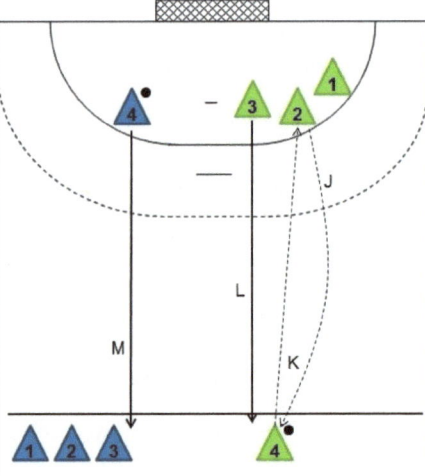

Define an exercise for the losing team before the game.

No. 44	Coordination sprint competition	8	★★
Equipment required:	2 coordination ladders, ball box with sufficient number of handballs		

Setting:
- Make two teams.

Course 1:

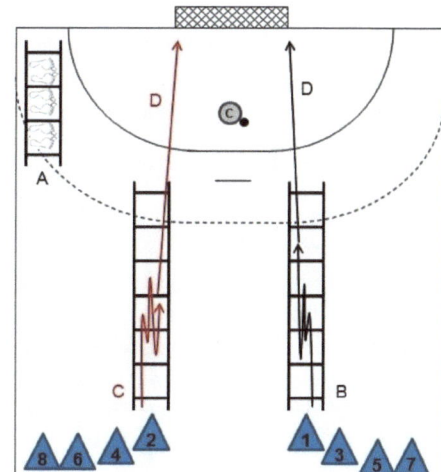

- 1 and 2 start simultaneously and sidestep (two steps per interspace) through the coordination ladders (A).
- 1 changes directions (B), 2 does the same (C). As soon as the coach bounces a ball, this is the sign for the players to sprint out of their coordination ladder (D/D).
- The player who first touches the goal post scores a point for his team.
- Afterwards, two new players start the same course.
- In the second round, the players switch tasks, i.e. 2 changes directions and 1 does the same.
- The team with the fewest points must do a predefined extra exercise at the end (10 quick jumping jacks, for example).

Course 2:

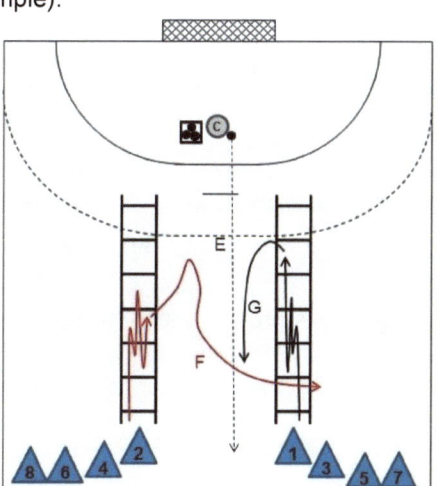

- Steps A-C from course 1 remain the same.
- Now the coach rolls a ball quickly between the two coordination ladders (E), which is the sign to start.
- As soon as the ball is rolling, the player who imitated the movements (here 2) starts and tries to sprint through his opponent's coordination ladder (F) without being touched by 1 (G).
- If 2 manages to run through the coordination ladder without being touched, he scores a point for his team.
- The players switch tasks again in the second round.

No. 45	Medicine ball transportation with sprint relay race	8	★★★
Equipment required:	2 medicine balls and 2 small vaulting boxes per 4 players, 4 cones		

Setting:
- Make teams of four.
- The players stand pairwise face-to-face, as shown in the figure.
- Each team gets a small vaulting box. Put a medicine ball on top of each box.
- Define tasks for the different ranks, the winning team does not have to do an exercise, the second team must do 10 straight jumps, the third team must do 20 push-ups, for example.

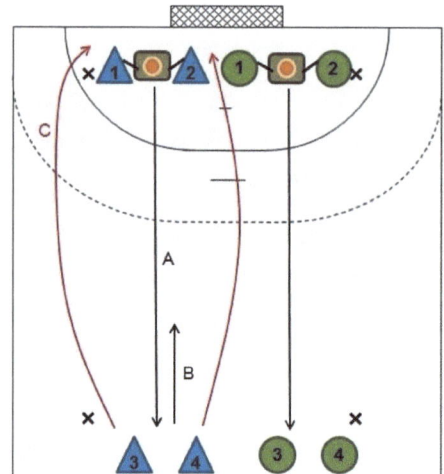

Course:
- The two players of a team lift their box with the medicine ball on top.
- On command, the teams of 2 run to the other side with their vaulting box (A). While doing this, they must make sure that the medicine ball does not fall down. If it falls down, the players must put down their box and put the medicine ball on top again before they are allowed to go on.
- As soon as they arrive on the other side, they put the box on the floor; the two other players take over the box and run back (B).
- The two players who first carried the box (1 and 2) run back on the side of the field once they have put the box down (without getting in the way of the other players carrying their box) (C) and take over the box again in order to carry it back to the other side. 3 and 4 also run to the other side etc.
- Repeat the course until each pair has carried the vaulting box to the other side 5 times (each team must carry the box 10 times from side to side).

⚠ For 3 to 4 teams, leave sufficient space between the cones so that there is enough room to hand over the box.

Ball throwing and transportation games

No. 46	Ball throwing competition	8	★
Equipment required:	14-20 handballs		

Setting:
- Make two teams. Each team gets a half of the court.
- Put 5 to 10 handballs into the center of each half of the court (team).

Course:
- Two players crisscross easily across their half of the court while passing a ball (A) (movements: forward, backward, sidestep).
- On command, both teams start to throw their balls from their half of the court into their opponents' half of the court (B). Each player is allowed to hold only one ball at a time.
- After 30 seconds (on command), the players stop. Count which team has the most balls in their half of the court. This team must do push-ups/sit-ups, for example.

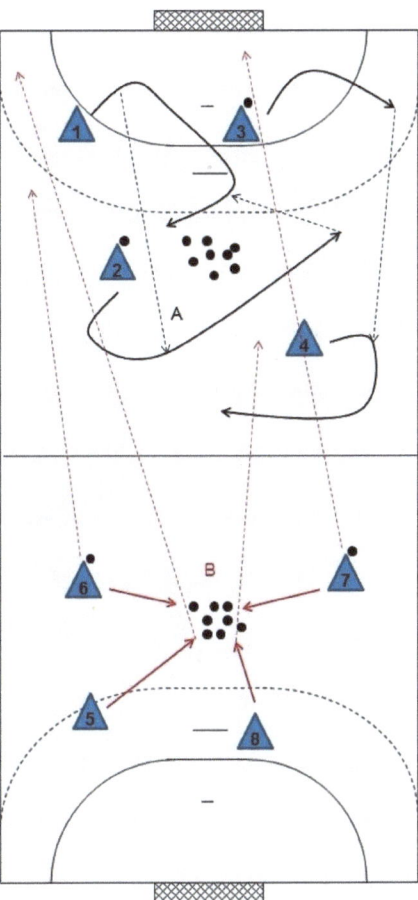

No. 47	Pushing the ball	6	★
Equipment required:	One handball per player, 5 medicine balls, 4 cones		

Setting:
- Define two lines with cones (or use existing lines).
- The players are divided into two teams. Each player has a handball.
- The teams stand behind the lines (one team per side).
- Put medicine balls on the floor between the defined lines.

Course:
- On command, both teams start and try to move the medicine balls across the opponents' line by aiming and shooting their handballs at the medicine balls.

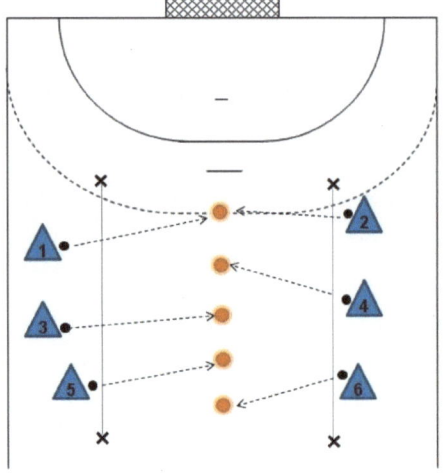

- The players may all shoot at the same time and at all the medicine balls.
- Once a medicine ball has crossed one of the lines completely, the players must not shoot at this medicine ball anymore.
- Which team has moved the most medicine balls into the opponents' playing field in the end?

⚠ Adjust the distance between the lines and the medicine balls to the players' level of performance.

No. 48	Transportation relay race	6	★
Equipment required:	6 small vaulting boxes, 2 small gym mats, 3 cones, 8 handballs		

Course:

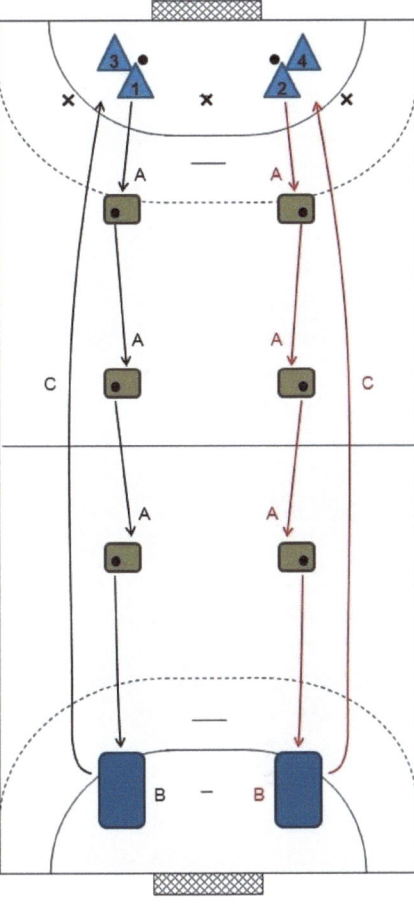

- 1 and 2 start simultaneously. They run to the first vaulting box while holding a ball.
- As soon as they have arrived, they put their ball on top of the box and take along the other ball on the box.
- The players repeat the course until they arrive at the third box (A). They take along this ball as well.
- The gym mat is the last stop. The players put the ball aside, do one (or more) push-up(s) (sit-ups, forward/backward somersault) (B), pick up the ball again, dribble back to the starting position (C), and hand over the ball to the next player.
- Keep going until each player has done the exercise.

⚠ The ball must not roll down from the box. If it rolls down, the player first must go back and put it on top of the box again.

The losing team must do push-ups or sit-ups ...

No. 49	Ball transportation and shooting	8	★
Equipment required:	2 soft foam balls, 2 ball boxes with 12-16 handballs, 2 cones		

Setting:
- Two teams.
- One player per team holds a soft foam ball.
- Position two ball boxes with 6 to 8 handballs each.

Course:
- Each team tries to put the balls from their box into their opponents' box within the given time. In order to do this, the players take the ball from their box (A), dribble to their opponents' box (B), and lay it inside (C).
- Afterwards, the players run back to their own box and pick up the next ball.
- One player per team (here 4 and 4) tries to hit the opponents with a soft foam ball (D). Players who have been hit must take the long way around one of the two cones (E).
- Who has the fewest balls in their box when time is over?
- The teams play several rounds (3 times 4 minutes). Change the foam ball player for every round.

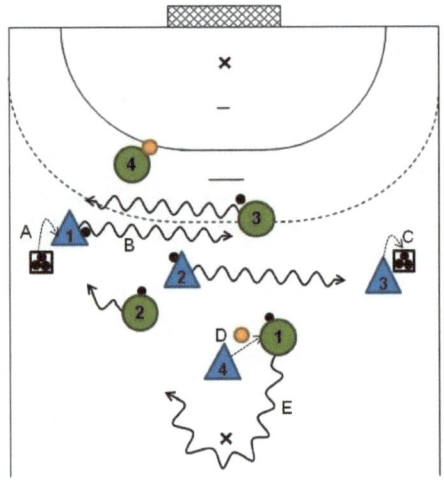

⚠ Pay attention to dribbling errors. If a player loses the ball or commits a dribbling error, he may have to take the long way around the cones as well.

Variants:
- Two or more players with a foam ball who may pass the ball and try to touch a dribbling opponent with it.

Competitive games for your everyday handball training
60 exercises for every age group

No. 50	Ball transportation by passing	12	★
Equipment required:	2 ball boxes, 8 cones		

Setting:
- Use the cones to define corridors (3 to 5, depending on the number of players).
- In each corridor, there are two defending players and three attacking players alternately (two attacking players are sufficient in the first corridor).

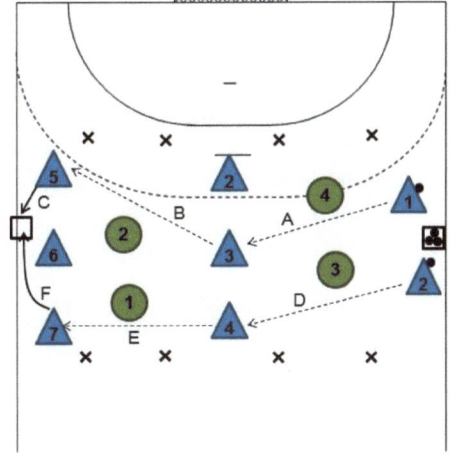

Course:
- The attacking players must pass all the balls from the ball box from one side to the other side and put them into the box as fast as possible.
- ① passes the first ball to an attacking player in the third corridor (A) who passes the ball to the final corridor (B) where the players finally lay the ball into the box (C).
- ② starts the same course (delayed; D, E, and F).
- Once he has played the pass, ① picks up a new ball etc.
- If the defending players steal a ball, they pass it back to the player who played the pass. This player may try again to pass the ball into the next corridor.
- Stop the time as soon as all the balls are in the target box. Afterwards, repeat the exercise with four new defending players and switch the tasks of the attacking players.
- Which defending team is able to block the attacking players for the longest time?

⚠ The players should quickly identify which attacking player in the next corridor is in the best position to receive a pass.

⚠ Maybe give the hint to feint a pass (so that the defending players run to the respective attacking player) and then pass to the free player.

Games from other types of sports

No. 51	Soccer in pairs	8	★★
Equipment required:	12 cones, 1 soccer ball		

Setting:
- Two players each hold hands. They are not allowed to let go.
- Position six cone goals on the playing field.
- The players play a soccer variant.

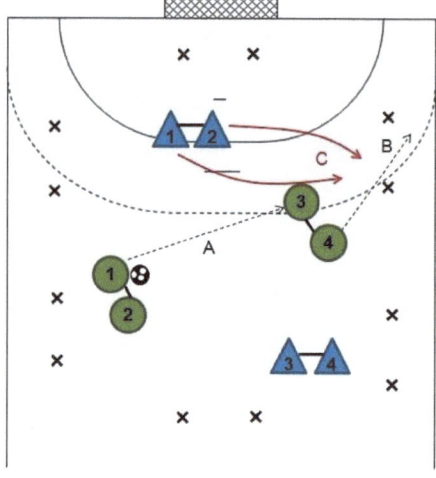

Course:
- ①② and ③④ try to kick the ball through one of the cone goals (A and B).
  If they score, they may keep on playing and score further goals. They must change the cone goal after each shooting attempt however.
- ①② and ③④ try to steal the ball and score goals themselves (C).

The team which has first scored 5 (10) goals wins. The other team must do an extra exercise (jumping jack, line sprints ...).

No. 52	No-look ball	6	★★
Equipment required:	2 bars, 2 large safety mats, 8 cones, 1 handball		

Setting:
- Make two teams.
- Position two bars next to each other on the center line. Put two large safety mats upright in between (with the long edge on the floor) so that the teams cannot see each other; see figure.
- Define two playing fields with cones in such a way that there is a 1 meter's distance to the mat.

Course:
- ① throws the ball over the mats (A).
- The team on the other side must catch the ball before it touches the ground (B) and throw the ball back etc.

Rules:
- When throwing the ball, the players must stand on the floor with both feet.
- If the ball bounces on the floor, the throwing team gets a point.
- If the ball bounces on the floor directly behind the mat (C) or if it is thrown out (D), the other team gets a point.
- The players must not leave their playing field in order to look which opponent currently has the ball, for example.
- The team which first scores 10 points wins the set. The teams play 3 (5) sets.

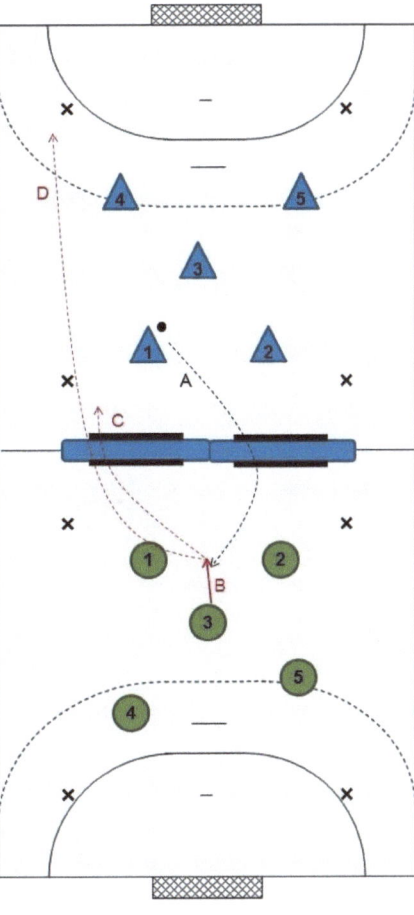

No. 53	2-on-2 intensive soccer variant	12	★★
Equipment required:	4 balance benches, 1 soccer ball		

Setting:
- Position four balance benches as shown in the figure. The seating surfaces must point towards the court (turned over by 90 degrees).
- Make two teams.
- The teams play soccer 2-on-2.
- The teams need to decide in which order their players are to enter the playing field.

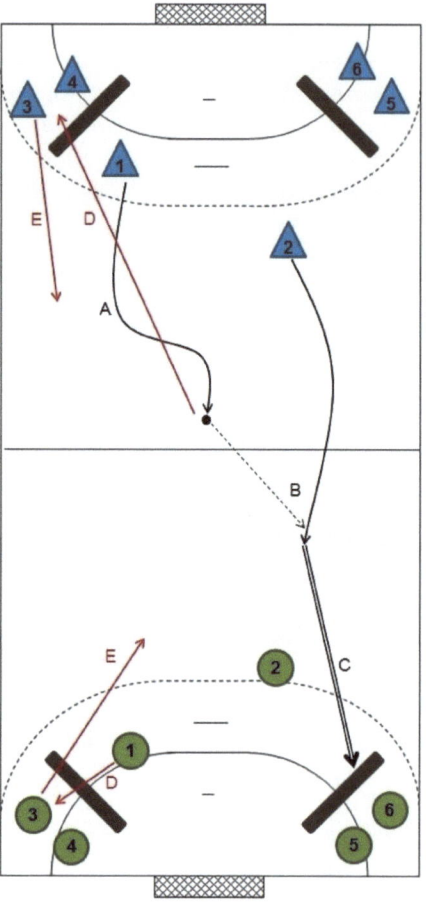

Course:
- 🔺1 and 🔺2 play against 🟢1 and 🟢2. They try to score by kicking the ball against the seating surface of the balance bench (A, B, and C).
- If a team scores, the four players 🔺1, 🔺2, 🟢1, and 🟢2 must leave the playing field at their balance bench immediately (D) (give a high-five). They are not allowed to enter the game again while leaving the playing field. One new player per balance bench is allowed to enter the playing field then (E).
- Now, 🔺3 and 🔺5 play against 🟢3 and 🟢5 until a team scores the next goal. The players then also leave the playing field at their balance bench, and so on.
- The players waiting outside to be substituted do both push-ups and sit-ups alternately during the waiting periods.

⚠️ For larger groups, play 4-on-4 (two players per balance bench).

No. 54	Endurance run with basketball	8	★★
Equipment required:	2 ball boxes with sufficient number of handballs, 4 cones, 2 basketball baskets		

Setting:
- Make two teams.
- Position two ball boxes at the center line and allocate a ball box to each team.
- Define the running path with cones (see figure).
- You need two basketball baskets, one basket per team.

Course:
- On command, 1 and 1 start simultaneously, run to the allocated ball box (A), and pick up a ball.
- They run to the basketball basket and try to score (B).
- Afterwards, they pick up the ball again and run around the cones (C).
- If they score, they may lay their ball into the opponents' ball box (D) and finish the running course (E and G). If the player does not score, he takes the ball along to the running course (F) and lines up again while holding the ball (G). As soon as it is the player's turn again, he uses this ball for his next round.
- 2 and 2 start as soon as 1 and 1 have thrown at the basket.
- Which team has the fewest balls in their box when time is over? This team is the winning team.

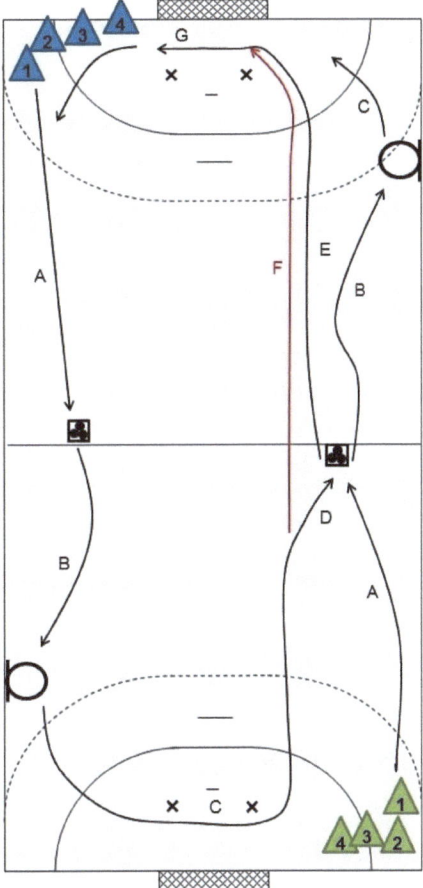

⚠ The players may do the running exercise twice for about 6 to 7 minutes; let them have a short break between each round.

No. 55	Dribbling-and-passing soccer	8	★★
Equipment required:	One handball per player, 1 soccer ball		

Setting:
- Each player holds a handball.

Course:
- The players play soccer across the entire playing field observing the following rules:
    - Each player must dribble his handball permanently.
    - The players must not hold their handball in their hands when kicking the soccer ball.
    - A player who loses his handball while dribbling/kicking is only allowed to reenter the game when he is dribbling his handball again.
    - There is no goalkeeper; the player who stands next to the goal may take up that role.

Variant:
- Each team has two handballs.
- Only the players holding a handball are allowed to enter the game (the players do not have to dribble the ball).
    - In the example, 4 passes the handball to 3 (A) who may now receive the soccer ball from 5 (B) and score a goal (C).
    - For example, the soccer ball must not be passed from 5 to 1 (D).
    - In the example, 3 may try to block 3's attack; 4 is not allowed to do so, since he has not yet received a ball.

Competitive games for your everyday handball training
60 exercises for every age group

Complex closing game variants

No. 56	Competition with defensive/offensive action	9	★★
Equipment required:	2 small vaulting boxes, 4 cones, ball box with sufficient number of handballs		

Basic setting:
- Two players each (①, ② and ①, ②) sit on a small vaulting box back-to-back. The two players sitting on the same box are a team during the further course.
- Put a ball in the center between the two cones.

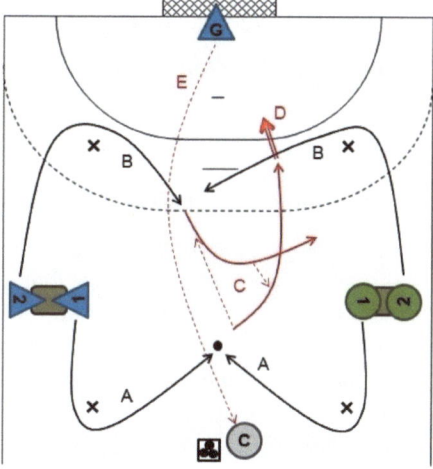

Course:
- On command, the four players start simultaneously (and the next four players sit down already so that there will not be a too long break).
- ① and ① run around their cone and each try to reach the ball first (A).
- ② and ② run around the cone in the back and then enter the game (B).
- The team which has won the ball now plays 2-on-2 against the two other players (C) and tries to score a goal (D).
- If the two defending players (① and ② in the example) manage to steal the ball, they may immediately try to score a goal themselves (they must play on the same goal). If they succeed, the other two players must do 10 push-ups.
- After the shot, the goalkeeper fetches the ball immediately and throws it to the coach/2nd goalkeeper who then lays it down at the initial position (E).
- And so on.

⚠️ The players may (should) discuss in advance who will fight for the ball.

⚠️ The players must adjust immediately if the defending players have stolen the ball.

No. 57	3-on-3 with running player	14	★★
Equipment required:	1 handball		

Course:
- Divide each team into two teams of three players each. ▲1, ▲2, ▲3 and ▲4, ▲5, ▲6 play together as well as ●1, ●2, ●3 and ●4, ●5, ●6.
- However, one player (here ▲6 and ●6) is the runner and may cross the center line (so that there is a 4-on-4 game in each field).
- If a team scores a goal, the goalkeeper does the throw-off from the goal; there is no throw-off on the center line as usual. Through this, the speed of the game increases significantly.
- To play a 4-on-4 game in the other half as well, two players of each team go into the other half of the playing field.
- Switch the playing fields after a couple of minutes.

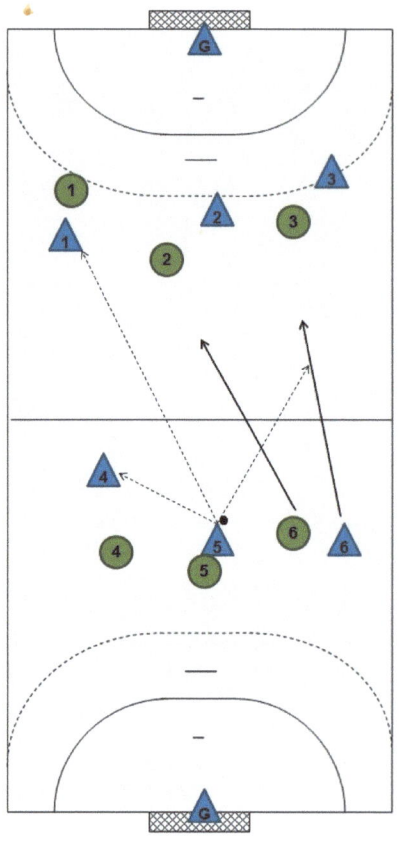

Objective:
The teams should quickly and independently identify which two players are in the ideal position to cross the center line. This will be different in each situation of the game. If a 5th player of the attacking team additionally crosses the center line, the other team wins the ball.

Variants:
- Without dribbling.
- Limit the number of passes to be played in each half of the playing field.

⚠ The teams are not allowed to define the runners beforehand, but must decide quickly, depending on the situation, who is in the best position to make up for the missing player.

⚠ The players must communicate and decide quickly who will cross the center line.

No. 58	Competition with defensive/offensive action 2	12	★★
Equipment required:	2 balance benches, 1 handball		

Basic setting:
- All players sit on two benches at the level of the center line.
- One handball lies on the center line.
- The players run on command. It is always the players before and after the called number who must run, for example:
    - The coach calls out "2" – 1, 3 and 1, 3 must do the exercise.
    - The coach calls out "5" – 1, 4 and 1, 4 must do the exercise.

Course:
- On the coach's command, the four players start and run to the goal line (define which team runs to which goal line beforehand) (A).
- Afterwards, they turn around and try to win the ball lying at the center line (B).
- The team winning the ball immediately starts an attack and tries to score a goal (C and D).
- The other team becomes the defense and defends against the two attacking players (E). If they manage to steal the ball, the players switch roles and may start an attack towards the other goal themselves.
- Afterwards, all players sit down on the bench again and the coach calls out the next number.

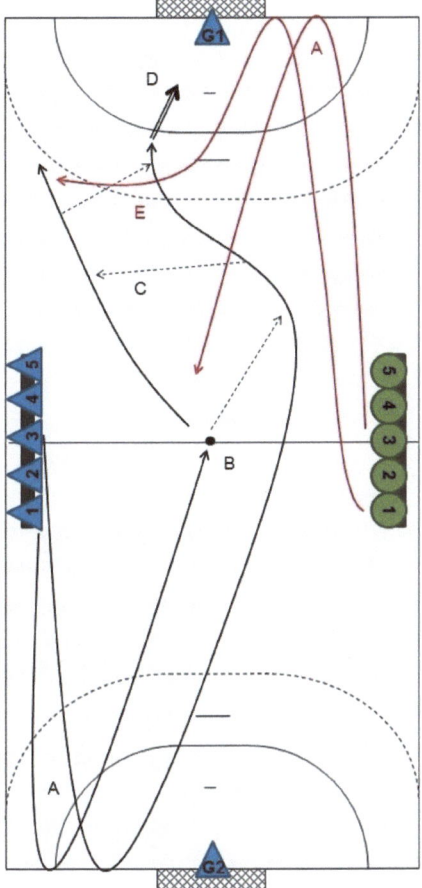

Variant:
- 3-on-3; for example, if the coach calls out "2", 1, 2, and 3 start.

Overall course:
- Define the playing time and count the goals scored. The losing team must do sit-ups.

No. 59	Handball with team completion	11	★★
Equipment required:	1 handball		

Course 1:

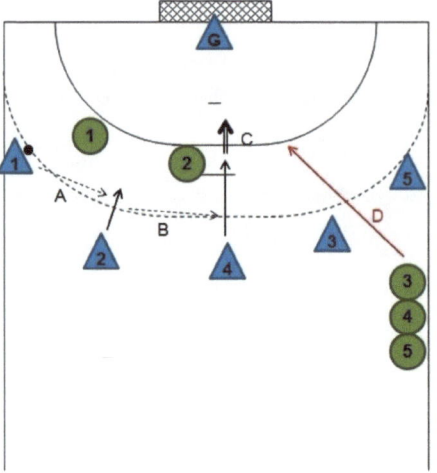

- Make two teams.
- The first team starts playing offense and plays an attack against 2 defense players (A, B, and C).
- If they score a goal, the next attack must be played against three defense players (D).
- If they do not score a goal, the next attack will be played against the same number of defense players as before.
- If they lose the ball due to a technical mistake or if the defense players steal the ball, one of the defense players leaves the playing field.
- The attacking players try to score a goal as fast as possible while there is an even number of defense players on the playing field. Measure the time and switch tasks afterwards.
- Which team scores faster when there is an even number of defense players?
- If a team is not able to fulfill the task within 5 minutes, switch tasks and write down the number of defense players on the playing field at the time of discontinuation.

Variants:
- Instead of measuring the time, you may also count the number of attacks needed to fulfill the task.

⚠ The team must fetch the ball themselves – the time keeps running.

No. 60	Beach handball variant	12	★★
Equipment required:	1 handball		

Setting:
- Two players of each team (2, 3 and 2, 4) as well as one goalkeeper per team stand in the field.
- The other players stand near the side line next to the playing field.

Course:
- 2 and 3 play 2-on-2 against 2 and 4.
- If a player leaves the field (A), another player may enter the field at another position (B), enter the game directly, and receive a pass (C).
- The defending players may also leave the field for tactical reasons (D) and substitute at another position (E) in order to interrupt the attack.
If the attacking players score a goal, the goalkeeper's pass is the throw-off. There is no throw-off at the center line.

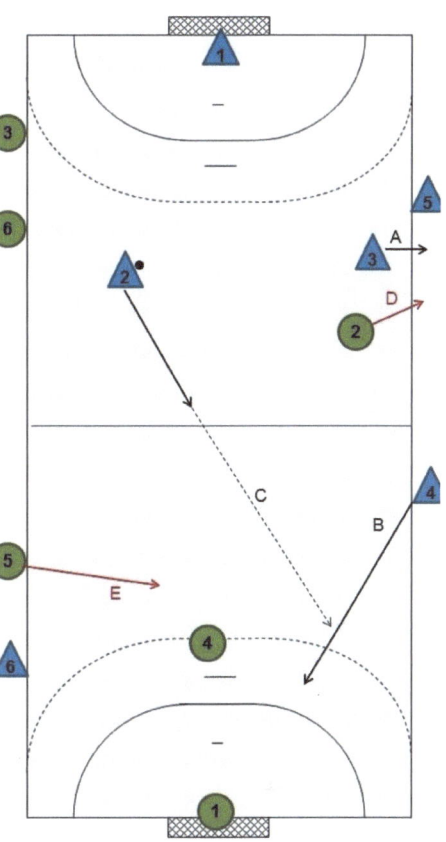

Rules for entering the playing field:
- If a third attacking player enters the playing field, ball possession switches immediately.
- If a third defending player enters the playing field, the attacking team may shoot a 7-meter penalty.

⚠ Before the game, allow the players a couple of minutes to discuss their substitution tactics.

Editor's note

In 1995, a friend convinced me to join him in coaching a handball youth team (male, under 13 years of age).

This was the beginning of my career as a team handball coach. Ever since I enjoyed working as a coach and had high requirements concerning my exercises. Soon, the standard pool of exercises wasn't enough for me anymore and I started to modify and develop drills myself.

Today, I coach a broad range of youth and adult teams with different performance levels and adjust my training units to the individual needs of the teams.

A few years ago, I started selling my exercises and drills online at handball-uebungen.de. Since, in handball training, there is a tendency towards a general athletic training that focuses on coordination work – especially in the training of youth teams –, a large number of my games and exercises can be applied to other sports as well.

Get inspired by the various game concepts, be creative, and rely on your own experiences!

Milestones of my career as a coach
- As of July 2012: A-License, DHB
- As of November 2011: Editor (handball-uebungen.de, Handball Practice, and Special Handball Practice)
- 2008-2010: Youth coordinator and youth coach, SG Leutershausen (Germany)
- Since 2006: B-License

Yours sincerely,

Jörg Madinger

Further reference books published by DV Concept

From warm-up to handball team play – 75 exercises for every handball training unit

By making your training units more diverse, you can increase the players' motivation, since you consistently offer new approaches to improve and refine familiar movement sequences. In this book, you will find inspiring exercises you can apply during each phase of your everyday team handball training – from warm-up and goalkeeper warm-up shooting to the common contents of the main phase and the closing games. Each exercise is illustrated and described in an easy, comprehensible manner. Specific notes give you tips on what you need to be aware of.

This book deals with the following key subjects:

Warm-up:
- Basic warm-up
- Short warm-up games
- Sprint contests
- Coordination
- Ball familiarization
- Goalkeeper warm-up shooting

Basic exercises, basic play, and target play:
- Offense/series of shots
- General offense
- Fast throw-off
- 1st and 2nd wave
- Defensive action
- Closing games
- Endurance

At the end of this book, you will find an entire methodological training unit. The objective of this training unit is to improve shooting and quick decision-making under pressure.

Handball for kiddies and young children under 9 years of age (5 training units)

Handball training for kiddies and young children is different from handball training for older players and considerably different from handball training for competitive players. During their first contact with "handball", kids should be familiarized with the ball in a playful way. They should be taught that being active, doing sports, playing together, and even playing against each other is fun.

This book contains a short introduction to handball for kiddies and young children and its special characteristics as well as example exercises which help to make your training units interesting and more diverse.

Following this, there are five complete training units of different difficulty levels that focus on the basic handball techniques (dribbling, passing, catching, shooting, and defending in a game with opponents). The kids are playfully introduced to the subsequent handball-specific basics. At the same time, particular attention is payed to general physical experience and the development of coordination skills.

The exercises are illustrated and described in an easy, comprehensible manner. They can be immediately integrated in every training unit. By using the given training variants, you can easily adjust the difficulty level of the training units to the respective target group. The variants should also encourage you to modify and further develop the exercises to make each training unit a new and more diverse experience for the children.

Passing and catching while moving – 60 exercises for each handball training unit

Passing and catching are two basic handball techniques which must be trained and improved continuously. These 60 practical exercises offer you various options to train passing and catching in a challenging and diverse manner. The exercises particularly focus on improving passing and catching skills even during highly dynamic movements. The drills therefore combine new running paths and movements similar to real game situations.

The exercises are illustrated and described in an easy, comprehensible manner. They can be immediately integrated in every training unit. Various difficulty and complexity levels allow for adjustment of the passing and catching drills to each age group.

Effective goalkeeper warm-up shooting – 60 exercises for every handball unit

Goalkeeper warm-up shooting is essential for almost every training unit. These 60 warm-up shooting exercises provide you with a variety of ideas to make the warm-up shooting challenging and diverse, both for the goalkeepers and the field players. The exercises particularly focus on improving the players' dynamics even during the warm-up shooting.

The exercises are illustrated and described in an easy, comprehensible manner. They can be immediately integrated in every training unit.

Whether you combine the exercises with additional coordination drills or use them as an introduction to the main part – various difficulty levels allow for adjustment of the warm-up shooting to each training unit and age group.

For further reference and e-books visit us at:
www.handball-uebungen.de

www.ingramcontent.com/pod-product-compliance
Lightning Source LLC
Chambersburg PA
CBHW041803160426
43191CB00001B/23